Black

By

Popular

Demand

Black

More Wit

By

and

Popular

Whimsy

Demand

ARTHUR BLACK

Published in paperback in 1995 by
Stoddart Publishing Co. Limited
34 Lesmill Road
Toronto, Canada
M3B 2T6
(416) 445-3333

Second printing May 1995

Hardcover edition published by Stoddart in 1993

Canadian Cataloguing in Publication Data

Black, Arthur
Black by popular demand : more wit and whimsy

ISBN 0-7737-5729-5

1. Canadian wit and humor (English).*   I. Title.

PS8553.L318B5 1993   C818'.5402   C93-094469-0
PR9199.3.B53B5 1993

Typesetting by Tony Gordon Ltd.

Printed in Canada

*Stoddart Publishing gratefully acknowledges the
support of the Canada Council, the Ontario Ministry
of Culture, Tourism, and Recreation, Ontario Arts
Council, and Ontario Publishing Centre in the
development of writing and publishing in Canada.*

*This book is reverentially dedicated
to Canada's eighteenth Prime Minister,
Martin Brian Mulroney,
for giving 27 million Canucks
what they need most from him:
a wave goodbye*

Contents

PART 3   *Do We Really Need This Stuff?*

PART 4   *Destination: TBA*

THE DOCTOR IS IN

(A Funny Thing Happened to Me on My Way to the Lakehead Agora . . .)

A S THE HOST of a somewhat eccentric radio program, I'm accustomed to finding myself in unusual situations. But this is one of my odder ones. A little bit uncomfortable too, if the truth be known. For one thing, I'm wearing my least favourite form of male protective coloration: a suit and tie.

Take my word for it — there's a suit and tie under here.

Over which I am wearing this billowy ensemble, which falls somewhere between a very expensive Japanese kimono and my mother's living-room drapes.

And then, of course, I am balancing precariously on my noggin something that has never balanced there before. The famous Cambridge bonnet, complete with tassel, which keeps dangling in my eyes.

Mind you, I'm not complaining. It's been a long time since I had anything fringe-like dangling in my eyes. At least I'm not alone. There are some three hundred fellow begowned and betasselled degree recipients here today, similarly dressed, similarly exhilarated, similarly, I am sure, trying to restrain the butterflies that appear to be playing cutthroat racquetball in our stomachs.

I want to get my confession out on the podium here before I see a platoon of Thunder Bay's finest come jackbooting across the stage to haul me away. I am a fraud. I confess it. I have no business wearing this cap or this gown or talking to these other gowned people here today. These people deserve their degrees. They've earned them. They've put in the years of hard work; they've forgone the new car and the dream vacation and the decent digs . . . spent the money on books and tuition and rent instead.

I didn't do any of that.

As a matter of fact, I never did much at all in the way of serious academic spadework. Two years of a three-year Ryerson journalism course, seven subjects of the mandatory eight required for Grade 13. Still carrying, as far as I know, though I haven't looked — Grade 11 algebra, Grade 10 economics, Grade 9 gym. I reckon I'd have to go all the way back to Grade 7 or 8 in Humber Heights Public School back about the time of the War of the Roses before I could turn up an actual certificate saying I passed something.

As soon as I found out the honour Lakehead University was about to confer on me, I phoned up my old pal Jake. Jake and I went to high school together. After we got out on the workforce we went into our separate drift patterns. Jake washed up in the foothills of the Rockies about twenty years ago and he's been there ever since.

"Hey, Jake!" I yelled into the telephone. "Lakehead University's going to give me an honorary doctorate." "A what?" my receiver grumped back at me. "An honorary doctorate!" I yelled. "An honorary degree of letters."

Long pause. Jake always was a master of timing. Then: "Expletive deleted, expletive deleted. The Doctor must be turning in his grave."

It was true. I hadn't thought much at all about the other Doctor since I suppose the last time he threw me out of his algebra class. But Jake's remark stirred the embers.

The Doctor had come to Canada from Hungary. His name was an unpronounceable glottal stew of consonants and vowels, but no matter. He made it clear from the first day that he expected to be addressed as the Doctor. We went along. He was the first Doctor most of us had seen who hadn't come attached to a black bag.

The Doctor also made it clear that he considered himself intended for much better things than this one-Doctor school in a one-horse Canadian town, drilling algebraic concepts into the Precambrian skulls of a bunch of thankless louts the likes of us. The Doctor combined a thick Magyar accent with a haphazard grasp of English that veered from Shakespearean to arithmetic — which made for interesting denunciations. "You een sag neef egg ance!" he would thunder at me. "You minoos quan tit tee. You zero factor! Go now from ziss chamber. Stand before de door, you young varlet, you."

The only time in my life I thought that I'd passed an algebra test was in the Doctor's class. I'd studied diligently, I was sure. I'd got a great mark — maybe even perfect. The Doctor handed back the graded tests in random order, intoning the marks as he went. "Jake Ree chard son . . . Sahvanty-vive pair cent," droned the Doctor. Good, I thought. Jake's dumber than I am in algebra. "Marry Jane Chepman . . . Sahvanty-nine pair cent . . . Artair Black . . . Eigh . . ." (In the eighties! Who'd believe it?) "teen pair cent."

Eighteen percent. Usually you know when you've booted an exam. Can you imagine how dumb you have to be to get eighteen percent in an exam you think you've aced?

Yes, I believe the Doctor might have a little trouble with this scene today.

I've always considered that mathematical moment of truth to be kind of the Crown Zircon in a lifetime of underachievement . . . but there have been other baubles on the charm bracelet of my life. Sales, for instance. I was the world's lousiest salesman. Men's wear, magazine subscriptions, newspaper advertising . . . I flogged it all, and moved nary a column inch.

Painter. I was a painter for one brief flowering creative period of my career. School gyms and washrooms, primarily — but also lifeboats, smokestacks, and other daubable features on the superstructure of a Liberian oil tanker I sailed on for one summer. Ah, how I remember that evening sailing through the Caribbean, the sun a great orange ball plunging behind the jagged humpback mountains of Jamaica, and the ship's bosun, a wiry, weathered old salt tattooed from his wrists to his earlobes. The grizzled bosun cast an expert eye over my day's work of painting. Put his foot on a stanchion, slung an arm around my shoulder, and murmured: "Have you thought of a career in sales?"

I tried teaching English and waiting on tables. I tried office work and stooking hay bales. I've plumbed and shingled, eavestroughed and ditch-dug.

And I've collected . . .

Pink slips, mostly.

What else . . . Been a cowpoke. I mean *really* a cowpoke. Poked cows down at the Ontario Public Stockyards in Toronto. There's a career challenge for you. On your first day at the Stockyards Indoctrination Seminar, a really tough-looking little Scottish guy swears at you for fifteen minutes, then presents you with your very own brand-new hickory cane, plus he makes you memorize the all-purpose cow command designed to get you out of virtually any dangerous bovine confrontation situation. I don't think the Affiliated Cowpokers and Bull Bunters of America would object if I revealed here before a live audience of university graduates that the all-purpose cow command is "*Ha*-Wagga-nagganaggahh!"

Sounds silly to us, but to a cow "*Ha*-Wagga-nagganaggahh!" translates as Bear to the Left Immediately.

It also means Bear to the Right, Back Up, Lie Down, and Get Off My Foot You Pathetic Sack of Hamburger on the Hoof.

Cows don't respond to vocal commands. That's why they give you the cane.

I tried a career in the movies once. Oh yes. I appeared in a Spanish opus entitled *Oscuros Suenos en Agosto*. Dark Dreams in August. I don't believe the English version of *Oscuros Suenos en Agosto* was ever released. I'm not entirely positive the Spanish version was ever released, but no matter. I had my celluloid moment. Picked me right off a street in Madrid, the casting director did. One doesn't want to be too bold in such situations, but I was curious. Pourquoi — you know — moi? Was it my Errol Flynn impishness? My Fred Astaire dexterity? My Bronsonian animal magnetism? No, said the casting director, it was my fluorescent green shirt. "You look like an American tourist," he explained.

You get the picture. Professionally, career-wise as they say, my life was a sad succession of buffetings and blunderings — until the fall of 1972. I was in Toronto. Had just been fired by the CBC. Well, correction. The CBC seldom fires people. They merely neglect to renew your contract. This saves CBC executives the embarrassment of using the f-word. But the rate of pay is identical.

In any case, there I was in Toronto, contemplating once again a future in sales . . . either encyclopedias or pencils in a cup. (Well, I know it sounds shabby, but I didn't plan to sell them as pencils. I intended to market them as hand-held, solar-powered word processors with a built-in delete function.) In any case, it wasn't necessary. I got a phone call from somebody named Doug Ward. How would I like to come and work at a radio station in Thunder Bay?

Well, I did what all Torontonians do when the words *Thunder Bay* first flicker across their consciousness. I dug out my Esso road map and flipped it backside up.

After discovering that Thunder Bay was somewhat farther north of Lake Simcoe than I'd imagined . . . I rented my house out, packed up my jalopy, and pointed the hood ornament north and west. Two days later, I was here.

It was not love at first sight. I got here in, I think, late September. The Lakehead sky was the colour of old gym socks. There was an ugly little snow squall scudding down May Street at times almost obscuring the neon winking come-ons from the fast-food joint and Blake's Funeral Home. I was nursing the first 50-cent cup of coffee I'd ever seen. Fifty cents for a coffee??? And I was thinking, "Doesn't feel like Eden so far."

But it did feel like a regular paycheque, and that was comforting so I stayed for a winter. Come spring, I tapped out a letter of resignation, had a series of goodbye beers and pointed my older, wiser, slightly frost-burned hood ornament south and east. I went to Toronto, back to my house. But it wasn't the same. Something had changed. I had been . . . there is no other word for it . . . *seduced* by the North.

I felt the way Mark Antony must have felt after Cleopatra flicked

7

a hip at him. Like Samson felt after he'd seen Delilah do the hully-gully. Toronto was still there. I was in bed with Toronto. Toronto was talking to me, cracking her gum, asking me why was I so moody. But I wasn't listening. Within six months I was back up north nibbling on the Lakehead's chilblained earlobe.

I stayed for thirteen years. Not a lifetime, but a long time. Thirteen years of signing off your radio commentary saying "I'm Arthur Black in Thunder Bay" creates a kind of permanence in the public mind, if there is such a beast. I haven't lived here for a dozen years, but still when I go to Vancouver, St. John's, Yellowknife, I'll meet people and they'll say something like, "Well, Arthur Black from Thunder Bay . . . How's the weather in the Lakehead?" I always tell them it's great. Thirteen years of talking to John Traine at Environment Canada taught me the value of the therapeutic falsehood.

I've been gone from the Lakehead now for some time. Long enough to look back and reflect on some of the things that make this part of the country forever unforgettable. The small things like Kangas, North America's most defiantly heterosexual public sauna . . . and things like Persians, the world's largest and most defiantly indigestible pastry. For those of you fortunate enough never to have seen a Persian bun, it looks like home plate slathered with pink stucco. And while we're on the subject of food — the Hoito . . . surely North America's largest and most venerable socialist restaurant. The Columbia Grill and Tavern, where waiters still hand you a pad and pencil and ask you to write your own order. Thunder Bay is the only town I know where failure to pass a literacy test can lead to starvation.

Ah, the Columbia Grill and Tavern! Hotbed of conniving municipal politicos and bored reporters alternately eavesdropping on the next table and contemplating a career move to a country station in Kenora. The Columbia Grill and Tavern, where if my timing had been better I could have hand-lettered my order for a Stan and Si sandwich and handed it to a fetching young waitperson who was wanted for Murder One south of Pigeon River.

Yep, if you just bided your time and toyed with the crumbs of your Persian long enough, all the big stories would come to you at the Columbia. Bambi Bembenek. Terry Fox. Yolanda Ballard. Walter Assef. Bobby Curtola.

When I first came to Thunder Bay I had trouble getting a handle on the place. I wasn't exactly sure how a city of 120,000 people was supposed to feel, but Thunder Bay didn't feel quite like it. Something was out of scale. I kept getting an image in my head of a young gangly hockey defenceman trying to skate in his younger brother's Cooperalls. I'm not sure, but I think it was Tom Miller who put it into perspective for me. He said: "Stop thinking of the place as a city of 120,000 people. Think of it as two warring tribal communities of 60,000 each."

That made sense for me. Port Arthur versus Fort William. However, I've heard the Montreal/Toronto jokes. I've spent time on the shuttle plane between Calgary and Edmonton. I've lived between Hamilton and Hogtown and I've followed the North–South conflict in Korea, Vietnam, Ireland, and Mason-Dixon . . . but I've never seen anything quite like the goings-on that go on between Port Arthur and Fort William.

The city was officially Thunder Bay by the time I came. I missed the real North–South rivalry by about a decade or so, but the air was still thick with folklore, myth, and legend. I heard all about the erstwhile Port Arthur fire and police departments and the Fort William fire and police departments, separate and identical, inviolate and indivisible, with the distance between their headquarters hardly more than the length of a decent fire hose. I was told about the take-no-prisoners hockey and base-ball rivalries between the towns, and the political sniping. The Fort William buses that stopped in the middle of a field so that you could disembark, produce your transfer, and board a Port Arthur bus parked in a field to continue your motor odyssey, which might be all of five minutes long. By the time I arrived one no longer had to set one's watch ahead one hour if one was travelling from one city core to the other, but the hairline fractures of urban exclusivity still ran deep. I remember stand-ing at a Keskus checkout desk with one North Ward oldtimer jawing about old Sodom on the Kaministiquia down the road. "Fort William?" he hooted. "Haven't been over there since just after the war."

I didn't have the nerve to ask which one.

Still, it was kind of a benign tension that expanded and contracted between the North and South wards, Port Arthur and Fort William. People lauded and applauded at least as much as they sniped and griped. Not much choice. In a northern city composed of roughly 14,000 Finlanders, 13,000 Italians, 6,000 Ukrainians, 5,000 French, and the rest of us a mongrel mix of native and immigrant Wasp and Jew, Catholic and Buddhist, Greek Orthodox and deconstructed Bush Hippie, it was pretty important that we get along. And of course we were all kept honest by the great outdoors, which here in the north is a natural phenomenon worthy of membership in the World Wrestling Federation. During my time in Thunder Bay, I often thought of Mother Nature as some huge, unlikely, over-steroided Valkyrie who sprang from her corner in early fall, body-slammed you to the permafrosted canvas, and didn't relax her death grip until midspring, when relieved by her tag team partner, Black Flies from Hell.

Ah, Thunder Bay. Long, hard winters, interminable ethnic bickering, blundering ineffectual government, two frosty solitudes . . . remind you of any country you know?

That's one of the beauties of a Lakehead University education: you got to live in Thunder Bay while you studied. Which means you've been forced in a kind of Precambrian crucible that stands as a microcosm for the larger Canadian experiment you now return to. What you've seen and witnessed in Thunder Bay, you will re-experience in Moose Jaw and Medicine Hat and Montreal and Musquodoboit . . . same melody written smaller or larger, louder or softer.

Well, I see my speech is slipping into what I call the avuncular perfect tense. I'm coming on like a kindly old uncle dispensing dollops of worldly wisdom to the assembled green of horn and tender of foot.

Nelson Algren advised: "Never eat at a place called Mom's, never play cards with a man named Doc, and never lie down beside anybody who's got more trouble than you."

But that's all book-learnin' advice. I'd like to leave you with a piece I figured out from personal experience. Here's my advice:

Before you pack up your bags and your wall posters and your diploma and head out of town, I would advise you to take a last drive up to Hillcrest Park overlooking the city on your last evening. I would further advise you to then sit down on the stone wall there by the ceremonial cannon, take a few deep breaths, drink in the grain elevators and the silhouette of the Sleeping Giant, and the lakers and the salties at anchor in the harbour . . . and the North and South wards spread out before you, resting peaceably under an electronic patchwork quilt.

And I would advise you to think long and hard about whether you really want to point your hood ornament anywhere.

I think it was Mae West who said, "I've been rich and I've been poor, and rich is better."

Well, I've been west and I've been east, and I never found anything better than what I found right here in Thunder Bay. I know, I know. There are economic realities and educational realities and there is also wanderlust and itchy feet and simple curiosity. A lot of you — most of you — are going to hit the road. That's okay.

All I'm advising is that before you go, see if you can't line up maybe some land-holding Lakeheader in Port Arthur or Fort William who's willing to rent you a corner of his garage or a bit of his attic. Someplace where you could leave a sleeping bag, a fishing pole, a pair of skis, maybe a "wasta" birch switch for Kangas and a book of dinner vouchers for the Hoito — just a stash for essential items in case you sometime feel an overpowering need to come back here and recharge.

One final piece of advice. Wherever you wind up, be sure to tell all strangers about the horrors of life in the Lakehead. Emphasize those eleven-month, eighty-below winters; play up the cannibalistic black-flies, the child-snatching ravens. Tell them about

11

the Finnish-Terrorist Ski Bombers, the unspeakable curse of Nanabijou. Tell them whatever it takes to scare them off.

That way, maybe we can keep Thunder Bay just the way it is.

PART 1

If We Can't Stop Progress, Could We at Least Scatter Some Thumbtacks?

The Snoring of Summer Lawns

P SST. HEY, MEESTER. Yes, you with the telltale green stains on your khakis. Come into my garden shed.

See that yellowed newspaper clipping thumbtacked to the wall? Right there, above those bags of pulverized lime, oxygenated bonemeal, kiln-dried peat, and deluxe organophosphate-enriched 21-7-7-lawn fertilizer?

Come closer and read the headline:

$7.7-MILLION DEAL SIGNED
FOR SLOW-GROWING GRASS

You can't make out the rest of the newspaper story anymore — the newsprint is too old and wrinkled. But that's okay, I know it by heart. It tells how Dr. Jan Weijer, a professor of genetics at the University of Alberta, has come up with a grass that grows so slowly homeowners need cut it only once a year. What's more, it requires little watering, no fertilizer, and it resists weeds.

The dateline on the newspaper clipping is January 1987. My first question is very simple. It's been six and a half years.

What happened?

Oh, how well I remember the day my eyes first beheld that glorious newspaper story. I fell to my knees in dewy-eyed bliss. (Truth to tell, I lowered myself gingerly — wonky knees from too many summers on dandelion patrol.)

A grass that had to be cut only once a year? A grass that

15

disdainfully tosses its myriad emerald heads at weeding and watering? Not to mention thrice-weekly infusions of Weed-B-Gon, Larva Lasher, Tuffy Turf, Plant Prod, and even pre-emergent Crabgrass Killer? Oh joy untrammelled! I have glimpsed Heaven and it is coloured Kentucky blue.

I've been fighting the Lawn Wars since I was tall enough to see over a scotch thistle. I've wielded garden shears, edgers, trimmers, push, electric, gas-engine mowers, and — my current war machine — a 12-horsepower lawn tractor with six forward gears and a cutting deck that can annihilate a swatch of grass 38 inches wide with a single whoosh of its wickedly whirling blades.

I've duelled through drought and flood, blight and infestation. I've gone *mano a* mandible with every creepy crawly from ear-wigs to white grubs. My second question is even simpler: Why do I bother?

Consider the inherent absurdity of the exercise. What good is The Lawn? As scenery it is featureless and monotone, and by definition, devoid of useful botanical perks like apple trees and tomato plants. While demanding at least as much labour and financial investment as a modest California vineyard, the lawn yields only grass, a bitterly inedible, unharvestable, surpass-ingly tedious crop fit only to serve as a flophouse for insects and a depository for itinerant canines suffering from distressed bowels.

But let us suppose that against all odds, one prevails. One coaxes and one coddles, one sweats and one spends and — *mirabile dictu!* — the damned thing grows. Then what?

Why, then one gets to cut The Lawn.

Forever.

Three times a week when it really hits its stride. Take a walk through any Canadian suburb some sunny Saturday midsummer afternoon. Such a stroll should be a tranquil, dozy, bucolic prom-enade. It's more like a running fire-fight in downtown Beirut. The air is blue-grey with exhaust fumes and the lawns are alive with bucking, whining, snarling lawnmowers jockeyed by overstressed homeowners plus the odd teenager not yet bright enough to fake a grass allergy. These people should all be snoozing, reading, making love, contemplating the galaxies in the underside of an oak leaf — even watching "Bowling for Dollars," for crying out loud. Instead they're hitched to those infernal suburban ploughs, engaged in that most useless and Sisyphean of twentieth-century quasi-pastoral rituals: cutting grass.

I am not sneering. I have no cause to. As I mentioned earlier, I've been a practising addict myself for more years than I care to reckon. Right up until that newspaper story about Jan Weijer and his wonder grass came along, and the scales (or maybe it was leaf blight) fell from my eyes.

Oh, I soldiered on. I continued to sod and fertilize and mulch and weed and cut and cut and cut and cut. But I did it with a song in my heart, knowing that soon this barbaric tradition would be history. Before long I would be hanging up my weed-eater, throwing away the keys to my garden tractor.

I fantasized about having my lawn sprinklers bronzed.

The summers shuffled by. No sign of the wonder grass.

This spring I scanned the garden catalogues with mounting panic. Still no sign of Weijer Grass. Finally, I snapped. I phoned the Genetics Department of the University of Alberta and asked to speak to Professor Weijer.

"He is no longer with us," a cool voice tells me.

Of course he's not! No doubt a platoon of Ninja assassins hired by the international lawnmower cartel have done him in! Five'll getcha ten his body lies buried under some unmarked tract of creeping red fescue in the Alberta foothills!

My paranoia is uncalled-for. The cool voice goes on to inform me that Dr. Weijer is retired and living on the outskirts of Edmonton. I call him up. A pleasant, courteous voice with a wisp of a Dutch accent curling around the edges tells me I am indeed speaking to "the Grass Doctor." I blurt out my question. His laugh tinkles gently over the phone line. "I'm afraid it will be a couple of years yet before you can buy the 'wonder grass,'" he says. "There's been a delay in getting the patent rights."

Well, I've lasted this long. I can do it. But now that I've reached the man whose discovery promises to unshackle every lawn owner in North America, I find myself chattering mindlessly to keep him on the line. I'm reluctant to let my grass guru go.

Idiotically, I ask him how his lawn is doing. That tinkling laugh again. "I've never liked lawns," says the voice on the phone. "I have four acres and they're covered with dandelions. Fields of gold. They are God's gift."

Stunned, I mumble goodbye and look out at my lawn. Hardly fields of gold, but patches of gold, certainly.

Definite potential.

Ah, it feels good to be just slightly ahead of one's time.

Woodsman, Square That Tree!

*We manipulate nature as if we were stuffing an
Alsatian goose. We create new forms of energy; we
make new elements; we kill crops; we wash brains.
I can hear them in the dark sharpening their lasers.*

A FELLOW BY THE NAME of Erwin Chargaff wrote that in a magazine called *Columbia Forum*. What amazes me is that he
wrote it more than twenty years ago, long before he could possibly
have heard of:

Somatotropin.

Square trees.

Egg advertising.

Nope, I didn't make any of those three things up. Scientists did.
And stories about their discoveries turned up in recent editions of
my newspaper.

Not on the front page, you understand. These aren't important
stories like Kim Campbell's latest pipe dream or an update on the
ongoing Mia/Woody soap opera, a.k.a. The Old and the Senseless.
No, these stories merely threaten to change the way you and I
live — hence their relegation to Section C, page 37, right next to
the truss ads.

Since we're in the ad department, let's take a look at the last
phenom first: egg advertising.

This brave leap forward comes to us from Golden Eggs Inc., an
Israeli company that claims to have perfected a method of imprint-
ing advertising slogans, brand names — even commercials —
onto the shells of regular, everyday store-bought eggs. Rafi Orel,

president of Golden Eggs, is ecstatic. "You can't ignore it when you open the refrigerator. It's shouting at you, 'Here I am!'"

Indeed. Just what I need when, bloodshot of eye and baggy of bathrobe, I groggily wrench open the fridge door in the predawn gloom: a chorus line of grade A medium ovoid Rockettes doing a cancan rendition called "Here I Am!"

How to find relief from my strident eggs — a quiet walk in the woods? Not likely. Robert Falls is busy in there, growing square trees.

Well, sure . . . just good business sense, when you think about it. Round trees are wasteful. When you turn 'em into straightened timber, about 40 percent of the log winds up on the sawmill floor. Scientist Falls has been monkeying around with saplings, stimulating them to grow extra wood cells at four points of their growth rings — squaring the circle, as it were. Says Falls, "Even if there's only a 5 percent increase, that would translate into millions of dollars."

Then there's somatotropin, a growth hormone Cornell University researchers say will do for cows' udders what stanozolol did for Ben Johnson's hamstrings. Somatotropin increases a cow's milk production by a whopping 25 to 30 percent.

There's an interesting double standard in play here: athletes caught using growth hormones are in disgrace. When Elsie the Cow shoots up, we feed the result to our kids.

Interesting economic theory in play here too: dairy farmers are already failing because of a glut of milk on the market. So we plan to goose the volume another 25 percent?

Square poplars. A hard-boiled egg in my breakfast egg cup with "BUY KODAK!" stamped on its shell. Weary Holsteins gushing milk like so many black-and-white fire hydrants.

You know, way back when eggs were tasty, milk was rich, and trees were in charge of themselves, a cartoonist by the name of Al Capp invented an animal called the Shmoo. Shmoos were about the size and shape of a bowling pin. They were friendly, bred like minks, and best of all, could become any kind of food you wanted, from flapjacks to filet mignon.

We've been herding and breeding and pruning and cross-pol-linating plants and animals for millennia. I think it's the Shmoo we've been after all along.

Of course, the Shmoo is nothing more than a fantasy. A cartoon invention.

So far.

Garlic Breath? What Garlic Breath?

I DON'T KNOW if I grew up in a deprived section of the country or not, but I never heard of or laid eyes on the mutant garden growth called zucchini until I was old enough to vote. It's strange when you think of it, because zucchinis are about the easiest green thing to grow this side of scum on a duck pond. You just throw a few seeds on the ground after the snow melts and before you know it, you've got zucchini the size of Lunenburg dories crashing through your garden fence. But we never planted them when I was a kid. Maybe we never bothered because somebody tasted a zucchini and decided, pretty as it was, there wasn't much point in growing something that had all the taste of a mulched telephone directory. We grew cucumbers in our garden. I believe that cucumbers are what zucchinis hope to be when they grow up. Zucchinis never do grow up, of course . . . they just become bigger zucchinis. Big and green and as mouthwatering as a mouthful of french-fried snow.

But that, oddly enough, makes them late-twentieth-century trendy, because tastelessness is in for food these days. We pass over delicious creamy golden-yellow butter in favour of some thin off-white oleaginous goop called "a spread." Everybody coos that health-wise it's much better for us than butter.

Maybe. But my taste buds don't think so.

Everywhere you look our food is being blandified. Good old greasy hamburgers have been eclipsed by lean, sensible (ugh) soyburgers. If Buddy DeSylva and Lew Brown were around today, they'd have to change the lyrics in their famous song to read:

"You're the non-aerated dairy creamer in my decaf,
you're the two percent in my Sanka."

Standard grub is being de-salted, de-caffeinated, de-fatted, and de-cholesterolled. Sure, the result is healthier, I guess, but for all the taste you get you might as well wear a woollen mitten over your tongue.

And now the latest: a British laboratory has announced (somewhat breathlessly) the invention of . . . odourless garlic.

Odourless garlic. Fine. One small nagging question. *Why?* Garlic is *supposed* to smell. That's how you know it's not a radish or a mushroom or a racquetball. Garlic stinks like Brett Hull scores goals. That's what it *does*.

Besides, there are some of us on this planet who do not find the smell of garlic all . . . that . . . unattractive. In fact . . . well, I'll let Tom Jaines say it for me. "I think it's a long time since the smell of garlic was considered unsexy among foodies. I can think of plenty of people it turns on." Tom Jaines said that, and he is not some wild-eyed Left Bank *Gitano* bouzouki-plucker. Jaines is editor of the much-respected *Good Food Guide*.

Nope. I've put up with zucchini and low-sodium minestrone. I've acquiesced to tofu and no-cal cola, light beer and cholesterol-free barbecue chips. But I draw the line at odourless garlic. I'm forming a Defenders of Garlic terrorist cell. Our motto: Garlic lovers of the world, unite; you have nothing to lose but your friends. Our secret password: the silent whistle. With apologies to Lauren Bacall: You know how to spot a garlic lover, don't you? Just put your lips together and blow.

If he doesn't fall over, he's one of ours.

Macho Nonscents

THE BURGUNDY BMW (vanity plate EGO 1) squeals to a stop directly in front of the No Parking Any Time sign. Vaulting from the driver's seat, a slim, tousle-haired businessman checks his Rolexed wrist, hefts a slim attaché case in one hand and a Toshiba laptop in the other as he jogs easily towards the glass doors leading to an exclusive-looking condominium tower. A liveried doorman opens the door, bows, and touches his cap to our hero, who flashes a Kennedyesque smile of acknowledgement.

"Have them wash the car, will you, Johnson? I'll need it again at seven-thirty." The young man, still smiling, disappears in a hiss of closing elevator doors.

Sound like anybody you know? Well, if he's not in your life now, he will be soon. Here's a little more data so you'll recognize the chap when he shows up:

He flies business class, likes Gershwin music, has a TV in his bathroom, and keeps his laptop in his study. He plays the stock market — and the field, having several amours on the go at all times. He also works out with a personal trainer and wears white Jockey briefs under those top-of-the-line custom-tailored suits.

This . . . person . . . is also, I am happy to report, the over-cooked figment of a gaggle of advertising copywriters working on the Chanel perfume account.

They made the guy up.

It's all part of a campaign to promote Egoiste, a brand-new perf— sorry, men's fragrance. According to a company spokesman,

Chanel's doing fine in the regular perfume trade. "The place left to develop the business is in the men's area."

Seems to me Chanel is a bit late off the mark. Brut, Old Spice, and Canoe have been trying to spiff up male spoor for a few decades at least, but better late than no show, I suppose.

Besides, it's not as if it's a flamingly radical idea or anything. Ancient Greek and Roman males routinely doused themselves with everything from cinnamon to oil of quince. The emperor Nero spent the equivalent of $200,000 on rose oils and rose petals for a single celebration.

The Roman Empire may have crumbled into ashes, but it smelled good on the way out. Romans had perfumes for their arms, perfumes for the hair, perfumes for the chest — even perfumes for the eyebrows. The elders of the up-and-coming Christian Church looked on with extreme and flinty disfavour. When the Roman Empire finally expired, so did the male perfume business.

And it pretty much stayed that way for several centuries. Now, Chanel hopes its new line, Egoiste, will reawaken the dormant dandy in us all.

I don't think it's going to work. Not for me, anyway. I don't know anybody like the mythical Chanel critter who opened this piece — and if I did, I wouldn't brag about it.

I think if men's perfumes are going to take off, perfume makers will have to offer more attractive essences. I don't know any guys who want to smell like tangerines, crushed almonds, or the scent gland of a civet cat.

Personally, I've never had any desire to smell like a spilled spice rack or an old English saddle, either.

No, what we need are perfumes that reflect manhood. Authentic aromas. Essential essences.

Plain common scents, if you will.

Such as . . . oh, I don't know — Eau de Lumberjack, perhaps? How about Truckers' Toilet Water? Cabbies' Cologne? I'm sure Toronto jocks would snap up Blue Jay Bath Salts — and I'll bet men's wear stores in Edmonton wouldn't be able to keep Eau de Oilers in stock.

There's a future for men's perfume, all right, but not for me. I won't be dabbing any Egoiste behind my ears or on the back of my wrists. Just the usual soap and water. The world will have to take me as I am.

Eau natural.

Breast Wishes

SAY WHAT YOU WILL about the dubious accomplishments of our age, but there was never another time in history when simple folk like you and I could walk into a doctor's office, flip through a colour chart in the waiting room, stop at the top of page 29, and tell the surgical nurse, "There! Those are the breasts I want."

Sure. Made-to-order breasts. Latest thing. Folks out there on the bowsprit of culture are quite blasé about it. The movie star Cher, for instance. Cher recently marched into a plastic surgeon's office on Harley Street in London and demanded that he examine her, then sign an affidavit attesting that "most" of Cher is the real thing. I'm not sure how Cher plans to use this information exactly. A discreet tattoo on her backside headed "Ingredients," perhaps? Doesn't matter. Point is, Cher was more than willing to own up to what she called the "usual" surgical enhancements, *viz.* a nose job and breast work.

Hey, don't laugh. It's you, not Cher, who's out of step here. Listen, there's a doctor in West Palm Beach who offers adjustable breasts for customers who can't make up their mind. A lot of women, he says, have second thoughts after breast implant surgery. They later wish they'd opted for larger implants. No problem when Dr. Hilton Becker's on the job. His implants can be reduced or expanded by adding or removing saline solution through a thin tube that can be tapped through the patient's armpit.

Adjustable breasts. What a Me-Generation idea! And surely just about as far as cosmetic chest surgery can go, wouldn't you say?

Well, not quite. You've perhaps forgotten about the other half of the human race? Men? They have breasts too, you know. And where you find breasts you find breast anxiety.

You may also find Gaston Schwarz, a Montreal plastic surgeon who is doing these days a booming business in busts.

Male busts. Dr. Schwarz can offer pretty much any kind of corporeal chassis remodelling that strikes your fancy, but of late, he finds more and more men are coming in and asking for the Pectoral Special. Artificial chest muscles that can be surgically implanted in the male chest in about one hour. They're not muscles at all, of course — they're bags of silicone gel. But they do the trick. They can turn a guy with a Woody Allen xylophone torso into a Conan clone, a Schwarzenegger lookalike. And all for only a couple of thousand dollars. Plus GST.

Well, I don't know. I guess Dr. Schwarz's patients have more bosom anxiety, more time, and certainly more discretionary income than I do. I think I'll continue to go with what God gave me. Not that I mock men who feel unfulfilled without a little thoracic enhancement. Heck, no.

Heaven knows, it takes a deep-chested fella to keep abreast of these times.

Dirty Hairy

I'LL BET YOU were asking yourself, "Gee, I wonder what's new in hair these days."

Well, sit'cherself down in my visitor's barber chair here, friend . . . you've come to the right place. I am a hair veteran. Been there and gone. I've lived through, if not actually cultivated: crew cuts, brush cuts, Iroquois cuts, college cuts, Beatle cuts, shag cuts, and Curly, Larry, and Moe cuts. I've seen my fellow man wear his hair in ponytails and Indian braids; in pompadours and the infamous D.A. — in which young males in heat did their level best to make the back of their heads look like a mallard's behind. The roof I live under may be thatchless now, but it's seen me through the Dry Look, the Wet Look, and the Eight Pounds of Wildroot Cream Oil Charlie Look, in which otherwise sane young men gobbed enough gunk on their locks to grease the retractable roof of the SkyDome.

Oh, I know hair. I've lived through spells of long hair, short hair, no hair, and purple hair. But even I, after a lifetime of tonsorial trend-spotting, would never have predicted the Age of . . . Dirty Hair.

It's true. The latest hairstyle rage is unwashed hair. Not unwashed forever. A couple of weeks, say. Just long enough to give it that lank, shingly look of a fur-bearing rodent drowning in a vat of Mazola. Dirty hair.

Why would anybody do that to the top of his head? To be trendy, of course. California hairdresser Victor Vidal explains,

"The whole look is eroticism. It's very animalistic. It's aggressive."
One of Mr. Vidal's hairstyling colleagues puts it more simply: "It's
a look," he says, "that says, 'Hey, I ride a Harley.'"

Or at least sleep under one with a leaky crankcase.

But what about people who've been, pardon the pun, condi-
tioned to shampooing regularly, yet still want to be "with it,"
hirsutely speaking? Not to worry, California capitalism is way
ahead of you. Enter Molding Mud, a new hair gel that's guaranteed
to make clean hair look dirty. A woman by the name of Jerl
Cusenza is the inventor of Molding Mud. She says she got her
inspiration from a homeless woman pushing a shopping cart
through the streets of Los Angeles. "I looked at this girl," says Ms.
Cusenza, "and I thought, that's just the kind of separation I want.
You know how street people don't wash their hair, and it has this
wonderful greasy texture?"

Couldn't agree more. I've always suspected homeless people
just do their hair like that for effect.

Molding Mud is selling like, well, like Wildroot Cream Oil used
to sell. Selling like hotcakes, but not to me, I'm afraid. I'm coasting
as always, a little ahead of the Hair Wave. I'm in another dimen-
sion, beyond dirty hair, long hair, short hair, purple hair. I dwell
in the Zen-like realm of . . . no hair. No gels for me. Or sprays or
conditioners or shampoos.

Mind you, for really special occasions I may use just a dab of
Mop & Glo.

Fit to Be Tied

M Y HERO OF THE WEEK? That's easy. Tom Stevenson, forty-five-year-old draftsman with the provincial tax office in Windsor, Ontario. I saw a photo of Tom in my newspaper recently, staring back at the camera with a goofy grin. And wearing one of the ugliest ties I have ever laid eyes on.

That's the whole point about Tom Stevenson — the ugly tie, I mean. He's got a closet full of 'em. Puce ones and chartreuse ones. Ties covered with psychedelic flowers and Day-Glo rainbows and neon vermicelli squiggles and squirts. He's got fishhead ties, hubba-hubba ties, ties that look like they were used to mop up in Chernobyl. Bastard tartan ties that would make Robbie Burns renounce his citizenship.

But the ugly ties are not so much adornments in Tom Stevenson's case. They're more like . . . armaments. Tom Stevenson has been going to work wearing the ugliest ties he could find each day for the past two and a half years.

Ever since the memo came down from head office decreeing that neckties were mandatory. Tom Stevenson hates neckties, as does any sane man. The necktie is an aberration and an abomination. All it does is fall in the consommé, get caught in the typewriter platen, and restrict the flow of blood to the head, thereby killing enough brain cells to make the idea of wearing a tie seem reasonable.

Ties started out reasonably enough. In the seventeenth century a regiment of Croatian mercenaries sported neckerchiefs, probably for the same reasons cowboys and pirates and navvies wore them — to keep out dust and, when wet, to cool the wearer down. Alas, the distinctive neckwear was spotted by England's Charles II, a noted fop and dandy. He adopted the Croatian neckwear for members of his court, along with the French name for the Croatian soldiers who wore them. The French called them *cravats* . . . the rest is sartorial history.

Those early cravats have multiplied and metamorphosed wildly. We have the Windsor, the four-in-hand, the puff, the ascot, the string, and the bowtie. Nooses, by any other name. Men have been voluntarily and enthusiastically throttling themselves with swatches of silk and cotton and manmade fibre for the past three hundred years.

Well, most of us have. Not Tom Stevenson. As I say, for two and a half years Tom showed up for work each morning with his neck festooned with the most repulsive piece of polyester money could buy. His bosses were unmoved. Finally, Tom did the unthinkable. He removed his tie on duty. He was sent home and docked a half day's pay. His union grieved — and won. An arbitrator declared the government-imposed dress code unreasonable. The mandatory tie rule has been poleaxed.

And rightly so. Once upon a time in a tony California dining room, a maitre d' stopped a customer. "I'm sorry, sir. You have no necktie."

"Don't be sorry," said the man. "I remember when I had no pants."

"I am sorry, sir," insisted the maitre d', "you cannot enter the dining room without a necktie."

The would-be diner spotted a bald man eating in the centre of the restaurant. "Look at him!" he yelled. "You won't let me in without a necktie, but you let him in without his hair."

The maitre d', like Tom Stevenson's bosses, was out of his depth. The tieless guy was Groucho Marx. Another hero of mine.

Costume Chaos

Fashion is a form of ugliness so intolerable that we have to alter it every six months.

— Oscar Wilde

MAYBE IT'S A LATE-BREAKING epidemic of spring fever, but Canadians are suddenly, inexplicably prattling about fashion, of all subjects.

This is an unexpected development from a people whose contributions to the world of high fashion to date are the tuque, mittens-on-a-string, and toe rubbers. Fashion plates we ain't. When it comes to fancy dressers, the Americans have Cher; we Canucks have Cher-ry.

As in Don.

But that, as I say, may all be changing. Suddenly, Canada is abuzz with fashion gossip. And it's getting louder.

First, it was the Mountie hats. A court decision decreeing that Sikhs could legally wear turbans while handing out parking tickets on horseback plunged the country into two bitterly divided camps. On the pro-choice side were the Canucks who thought that turbans were fine — and while we're at it, why not bicycle helmets, yarmulkes, feathered headdresses, Raiders-of-the-Lost-Ark fedoras, and beanies-with-propellers too?

These Bolshevik faddists were strenuously opposed by the Traditionalists — staunch, loyal patriots who liked the Mountie hat just the way it was, thank you very much.

If I understand the kernel of the Traditionalist position, it's "if the hat is good enough for Yogi Bear it's good enough, by God, for Canada's finest."

But the Mountie hat is not the only brush fire on the fashion front. Ed Werenich has joined the fray as well. A while back, on his way to the World Curling Championship, Ed got his rocks off about the deteriorating dress codes for curlers.

Dress codes for curlers? Is this a David Letterman sketch?

Nope, Ed was serious. He hates those track suits that European curling teams wear. "It's like a pyjama party. They look like they should be out jogging instead of curling." The Canadian skip favours the time-honoured sweater-and-pleated-slacks approach.

Well, whether or not you agree with him, you have to admire Ed's chutzpah. Here's a guy with the silhouette of a municipal water tank telling us what's chic and what is not.

I'm not saying that Ed is unduly chunky . . . but he is the only member of the Canadian Men's Curling Team who was forced to wear a T-shirt with the message "I Am Not the Zamboni, Please Get Off My Back."

And as if fashion uncertainty on the curling sheets and in the Mountie's saddles of the nation wasn't turmoil enough, we've got vogue vagueness in the Post Office as well.

A while back Canada Post nabobs unveiled their all-new Posties on the Job fashion line. Were the 27,000 new uniforms (trousers, shorts, jackets, and baseball caps, all in acrylic royal blue) a critical hit? Well, they took the Canadian Union of Postal Workers' collective breath away.

Most of it, anyway. The posties still had enough wind left to say words like "ugly," "baggy," "synthetic," and "clownish."

"Most people could leave the Post Office and start working at Burger King without changing clothes," said one official. Looking sideways at the transparent-when-wet top, a female letter carrier commented, "I'm not too fond of entering wet T-shirt contests."

Ah, me. Costume quandary and uniform uproar everywhere you look, these days. Personally, I don't know what the Mounties, Ed Werenich, and the posties are whining about. Those new get-ups aren't so bad. Somebody should tell 'em to straighten up and stop complaining or we'll hit them with some truly hideous uniforms.

Let's see, now. The Vancouver Canucks are out of the playoffs, aren't they?

Don't Let the Stars Get in Your Eyes

Put three grains of sand inside a vast cathedral, and the cathedral will be more closely packed with sand than space is with stars.

— Sir James Jeans

A WONDERFUL COMMODITY, SPACE. As someone once pointed out, without space, all matter would be jammed together in one lump — and that lump wouldn't take up any room.

Of course, space is a very relative commodity. There's more of it between atoms of balsa than between atoms of mahogany. More on a hockey rink than on a chess board. More between residents of Tuktoyaktuk than between residents of Tokyo.

And then there's outer space. These cold, clear winter nights are perfect for gazing up at the sky and rediscovering the real meaning of space. It's the same wide-screen extravaganza, unreeling night after night. Your grandparents watched it. So did Mackenzie King and Champlain and Shakespeare and Cleopatra and Moses and Methuselah, all the way back to those nameless, heavy-browed shuffling ancestors of yours and mine, huddling in caves, fearfully peering out at the nocturnal spill of jewels across the sky.

It's a very humbling experience, looking at the night sky. It's one of the few things mankind hasn't managed to alter or desecrate. I sometimes think that if our former leader had spent more time levering his massive mandibles skyward and less time rolling dice in the back room, Canada might not be in the mess it's in. But politicians tend to cluster in cities, and light pollution makes cities the worst place to stargaze.

In any case, ten minutes of uninterrupted stargazing makes Canadian politics seem farther away than Jupiter.

I haven't managed to pick them out yet, but I understand there are four newly named asteroids winging around up there. They used to orbit under the stunningly boring names of Asteroid 4147, 4148, 4149, and 4150, but astronomers in a playful mood decided to rechristen them Lennon, McCartney, Harrison, and Starr.

That's right — the Beatles in outer space.

Sort of . . . loosely in the sky like diamonds.

It's not often you'll catch astronomers in a playful mood. They are, by and large, a solemn bunch. And if you ever want to catch them at their grim and grumpy worst, ask astronomers what they think of astrologers.

"Pure hokum!" they'll snap. "Utter nonsense!"

Astronomers have no use for a people who predict the future by eyeballing the arrangement of the planets.

Astronomers can produce roomfuls of data to prove that astrology and horoscopes are just a crock of moonshine. Problem is, most folks don't want to hear it. Eighteen hundred daily newspapers on this continent carry horoscopes. Editors claim it's invariably one of the most popular features. One Gallup poll discovered that 55 percent of North American teenagers believe that the position of Venus vis-à-vis Saturn will determine their chances at the Saturday night dance.

And it's not just North American teenagers. In the East, politicians and businesspeople regularly consult astrologers for help in selecting auspicious dates to launch new enterprises. In Korea, China, and Japan, it's the neighbourhood soothsayer who gives the final nod for wedding days.

My favourite quote on astrology comes from a New York City detective whose job it was to bust fortune-tellers for operating without a licence. "I've gone into hundreds of fortune-tellers' parlours," she recalled, "and I've been told thousands of things, but no astrologer ever predicted that I was a policewoman getting ready to arrest her."

So I guess when it comes to astrology, you can put me down as suspicious.

But then you know what we Virgos are like.

Forging Fatness into Fitness

I DON'T KNOW HOW you plan to remember the eighties, but for me it will go down as the Decade of Exercise Excess.

The dubious pastime of whipping suet-y human carcasses into something approaching perfection gained cult status in those ten years. Perhaps it was because so many baby boomers hit middle age all at once and discovered simultaneously that it had been a long time since they'd had visual, first-hand evidence of anything below their navels. Personally, I got tired of hearing my chins applaud every time I crossed a set of railroad tracks. Whatever the motivation, a lot of folks volunteered to work up a sweat, and the eighties was definitely the decade to do it in. The eighties gave us the Jane Fonda videos, power walking, leg warmers, and a television phenomenon in which nubile bunnies hopped and puffed and rrrreached and strrretched accompanied by fluffy instrumental music and wearing nothing but a swatch of spandex and a brainless smile.

The eighties taught us that someone running through the park in the predawn gloom was not necessarily a peeping tom in full flight; that a man jogging on the spot at a downtown intersection sweating profusely and wearing a black Lycra body suit was not necessarily a purse snatcher or a cat burglar.

These people were not felons. They were Shining Exemplars. Heroes to be admired and emulated. They were worshipping at the Temples of their Bodies. And considering what the Swaggarts and Robertses and the Bakkers were doing under the altars of the regular churches, old Corpus United didn't seem like a bad place to bend our knee in the eighties.

Yessir, the eighties was the decade in which a lot of Canadian couch potatoes decided they were tired of being unable to cut the mustard as well as a sixty-year-old Swede. So we dug out those high-school runners from the back of the closet and resolved to Shape Up. But once we had those runners laced and we'd stuffed ourselves into a pair of track pants, we had a problem: where to go to — you know — get perfect? Nobody wanted to expose their physiological imperfections to the world by jiggling around the local high-school running track or wheezing through a creaky set of push-ups on the lawn.

Fear not. The eighties had the answer.

The Fitness Club.

Oh, sure, fitness clubs have been around for a long, long time, but they really came into their own in the eighties. The old clubs had been, as a rule, slightly seedy, smelling of sweat and liniment, presided over by a bald guy who smoked cheap cigars, handed out towels, and answered to Knobby.

In the eighties the fitness clubs went yuppy. Gone were the clanky old barbells and punching bags haemorrhaging sawdust. In their place were very shiny, very expensive machines. Machines that were good for nothing but exercise.

Man used to tote that barge and lift that bale. In the eighties he worked out on a Nautilus. We used to take Sunday afternoon bike rides or row around the bay. Now we wait in line to work up a sweat on stationary bikes and rowing machines.

And then there's the Life Fitness Lifestep Model 300X. It's as shiny as a Nautilus, as sleek as a stationary bike, and even trendier than those rowing machines that don't go anywhere. It features padded foot pedals, adjustable hand grips, variable drive, and a computerized LED screen for continuous feedback on your progress.

Wanna know what you actually *do* on the Lifestep Model 300X? Well, you, ummm . . . climb steps.

That's it! You just climb a set of steps that keep rotating so that you can climb them some more.

You can do the same thing every lunch hour climbing the stairs at work. Well, why not? Simpler is usually Better. Doctors now say the best overall exercise isn't sprinting or pumping iron or marathon swimming — it's walking. Fun, too. No overpriced outfit to buy, no membership dues, no locker combination to remember. A brisk walk gives you fresh air, a change of scenery, a good cardiovascular workout, plus, if your route takes you past a fitness club with windows . . .

Your morning chuckle.

Grumps of the World, Unite

Y OU HAVE A FAVOURITE pair of jeans? I do. Keep 'em on a hanger in my cupboard. They've got that washed-out smoky-blue pastel look and the puppy-nose velvet texture that jeans get after you've washed them about eleven million times. I've had these jeans since the last Ice Age. They're classics. Low rise, flared leg. And I can still get them on.

Pretty well. I can zip the fly right up as long as I don't breathe out, and my belt covers the, uh, gap between the top button and the top buttonhole. I'd be proud to be seen in these jeans down-town any Saturday night. If I hadn't seen myself in the bedroom mirror last night.

I look like a double-dip strawberry in a blue denim cone.

Hey, I'd feel bad about it if I didn't know that I was on the cutting edge of a trend. Sure! Most of my peers are getting the same bad news from their bedroom mirrors these days. Apart from a very few anorexic anomalies like Princess Di and Jane Fonda, most of us lean, hard sixties folks aren't so lean and hard anymore.

It's the nineties now and we're . . . well, we're bald or grey and double-chinned and a little short of breath and definitely thick through the waist and, umm, less than taut on the bottom.

There's a lot of us. In fact, there are whole marketplaces full of us. We're so numerous that the advertising world has a name for us. They call us grumps.

That's G.R.U.M.P. — stands for Grown Up Mature Profession-als. We baby boomers are beginning to show our age. The law of gravity is winning. And the folks who sold us stuff when we looked lean and mean are standing by to sell us a whole new range of things to accommodate our newer, droopier selves.

Have you seen the new jeans available from Levi's and Lees? Unabashedly loose in the thigh and baggy in the bum. "Forget about cholesterol," one TV ad trumpets, "it's your jeans that have been cutting off your circulation."

Well, I can live with this. I never liked skin-tight jeans even when I had tight skin.

Another unexpected plus of being a Grump is that one gets to be a guest at the funeral of — hurray — jogging. Oh, jogging will flip-flop on its deathbed for several more years as young folks plod, purple and sweating, up and down the highway shoulders of the nation. But the backbone of the jogging industry — the baby boomers — has reached an age where knees creak and lungs wheeze and hammering hearts cry out, *Are you serious?* Proof of jogging's demise? Running shoe sales have bottomed out in the past few years.

Not that shoe sellers are hurting. They just adjusted their sights and started selling footwear aimed at a slower, less energetic consumer — *viz.* the Grump. Shoemakers are now selling six times as many *walking* shoes as they were in 1986. Yes, friends, we live in an age when consumers line up to pay good money, and plenty of it, for shoes — but only if they're good for walking, mind.

Ah, well. It's not the first time I've been taken in by footwear. There's a cardboard box in my cupboard right under my blue jeans. It's full of shoes I no longer wear. Thongs. Hush Puppies. Desert boots. Earth shoes. Remember Earth shoes? The ones that made you walk uphill all the time?

Someday I plan to write a book about my meander through the fashion world of the late twentieth century.

I think I'll call it *Gullible's Travels.*

These Shoes Were Made for Walking

S O THERE I AM, hiking along the Bruce Trail through a delightful southern Ontario hardwood bush. Lofty beech and oak and maples vaulting over my head, competing for solar attention. Blue jays, chickadees, and flickers skittering through the air. Bucolic countryside panoramas undulating out to port and starboard like huge billowy comforters stitched by Grandma Moses. Stimulating conversation from my fellow hikers, who are strung out on the path single file, fore and aft. I am following a woman who buys her jeans on the tightish side, from Wrangler.

And am I taking any of this in — the atmosphere? The conversation? The scenery? No, I am not. Because I am preoccupied.

I cannot take my eyes off the feet of the woman in front of me.

Actually, it's what's on her feet that has me mesmerized. They must be shoes because that's where shoes go, right? And anyway, it says NIKE in big bold letters right across the back.

But has the world ever seen shoes like these? They are orange and white with lightning streaks of psychedelic mauve down the side. They feature batwing tabs and Velcro lugs and a huge padded tongue, and the footprints they make on the trail look like something left by a John Deere tire. These shoes are an acid flashback. They're the kind of product you'd get if Hunter S. Thompson took up the shoemaking trade. I quicken my pace and catch up to the Nike maiden. "Nice running shoes," I lie brazenly.

"They are not running shoes," she tells me, somewhat huffily. "They are walking shoes."

Oh, of course. Walking shoes. How myopic of me. We live in a world that has shoes for basketball, racquetball, cycling, tennis, jogging, sprinting, marathons, rockclimbing, and windsurfing. We can purchase shoes that feature pronation stabilizers and Achilles massagers — not to mention nitrogen compression chambers, thermoplastic arch balloons, elevation pumps, and carbon-fibre power feedback systems. We've got shoes with all that. I'd say the world is overdue for . . . the *walking* shoe, wouldn't you?

How did it come to this? Whatever happened to Less Is More? Remember back in the sixties when people spent their money on headbands instead of haircuts? When they shopped at the Sally Ann and drove Bugs? When it was okay to wear T-shirts and duffel coats and serapes and rope sandals? How did we ever get from that to $200 Airwalks?

I don't know, but I am delighted to report the sighting of an old friend this week. Remember Gazelles? Maybe not. Gazelles were a cheap, low-slung, pebble-bottomed running shoe made by Adidas back in the seventies, long before the athletic footwear industry was born. Gazelles had no pumps, no Velcro straps, no magic cylinders. They were just plain running shoes. In the tradition of Henry Ford's original Model T's, you could have 'em in any colour you liked, as long as it was blue and white. Well, Gazelles are back. I saw them in a shop window last week. Soon as I get my paycheque I'm going to go back and get me a pair. Why not? They're not fancy, but I'm sure they'll do for everything I need.

Why, I wouldn't be surprised if you could even walk in them.

Forget the Black Plague — What about Aerobic Ear?

IT SOUNDS A TAD perverse, but I find myself longing for the days of simple killer diseases. Our grandparents grew up in a very simple world, affliction-wise. There was cholera, polio, typhus, malaria, consumption. Minor-league maladies included chicken pox, scarlet fever, measles (red or German), and mumps. And that, aside from the odd unscheduled bout of appendicitis or diphtheria, was pretty well it for life-threatening situations. Simple straightforward honest diseases that everybody knew and feared.

But nowadays? Nowadays it seems as if there must be an entire government department squirrelled away in Ottawa or Washington whose whole reason for existence is the discovery of new things that might kill us. Have you heard about some of the new contagions? Like Tortilla Chip Tear? It's an occupational hazard for grazing couch potatoes. First reported case was an Arizona woman hospitalized for repairs to a gash in her esophagus — caused by swallowing an insufficiently chewed tortilla corn chip.

The irony about many of these new maladies is that they often strike folks who are trying to exercise their way to fitness. Bowling Plexopathy is one. That's throbbing pain in the neck and shoulders often accompanied by numbness of the thumb and forefinger caused by too much you guessed it. There is also Dog Walker's Elbow, which you contract by being leashed to a dog that suddenly spies a cat and yanks the leashed arm half out of its socket. And Aerobic Ear. This is a condition of prolonged dizziness and hearing loss that is showing up among aerobics instructors. Doctors think the combination of dopey jumping and dopey loud music that *is* aerobics may be jarring the balance mechanisms in the instructors' inner ears. Whatever . . . there are more and more aerobics instructors out there who are saying "Pardon?" And falling down a lot.

Well, a cynic would say that anyone who goes out and exercises is just asking for trouble, but the bad news about the new infirmities is you don't have to go *out* and get them. Even if you just sit on your chesterfield watching TV, they'll come and get you. In fact, especially if you watch TV. The *New England Journal of Medicine* reports the case of a woman who gets epileptic seizures every time she sees Mary Hart, the co-host of "Entertainment Tonight," on TV.

This Mary Hart disease is so new they don't know what to call it. Hart Attack? Marylaria? Cohostophobia?

And how do you treat a problem like that? Give the woman tiny doses of Geraldo Rivera and old Jerry Lewis movies until she builds up sufficient antibodies to handle Mary Hart?

There is an easier cure, of course. I prescribe giving up television. Stick to radio. It's much easier on the eyes, and the people you hear are as pleasant as your imagination can make them.

But if you insist on eating tortilla corn chips while listening to radio, remember: Chew each mouthful thirty times, okay?

Radio. Remember our motto: We haven't killed anyone yet.

PART 2

Get a Job!

How to Impress the Boss

A LOT OF READERS THINK I spend all my waking hours in a roach-infested flophouse garret, drinking cheap wine and eating mouldy heels of baguettes when I'm not throwing myself at the walls trying to come up with an idea for my next newspaper column.

Not true. Once in a while I slip down to the local radio station to host a weekly radio show. (The station could be described as a roach-infested flophouse, but that's another horror story.)

The reason I bring up my Other Life is that my producer recently interviewed applicants for a research job on our radio show.

I found him the morning after, face down on his desk blotter, whimpering quietly.

The job interviews had not gone well.

The first applicant who showed up was a chirpy, energetic woman with more questions than answers. "This program — it's kinda like a current affairs type program, isn't it?" Well, no, said my producer, not exactly. He asked the job-seeker if she ever listened to the program. "Afraid not," she replied. "I mostly just watch TV."

The next hopeful was a breezy, affable guy wearing a sportsjacket that could halt traffic and a pinkie ring that Curtis Strange could have teed off on. He cruised through the office doors and hove to in front of a woman he took to be the receptionist. After eyeballing her approvingly from stem to gudgeon, he murmered, "Hi, doll, is the boss in?"

Alas for Lothario, "doll" was the boss. Director of the department and a woman whose subscription to *Ms.* magazine has not lapsed. She asked icily if he treated all female office workers as personal flunkies. The guy, already up to his neck, dug deeper.

"Hey, lady, no way. I know you gals are *every*where these days!"

And so it went. The applicants for the job grew more and more unsuitable, my producer grew more and more dismal.

I could have taken him out for a drink. I might have fixed him up with a pair of mid-stripe tickets for the next CFL game. But I did something much more appropriate.

I went out and got a copy of the Robert Half survey.

Robert Half International is a well-known American firm that recruits executive and professional help for companies in the financial industry. Recently they contacted the personnel directors of a hundred major corporations and asked them one simple question: What was the most unusual job interview you ever conducted?

The responses were more astounding and hilarious than the folks at Robert Half International could have hoped for. Personnel directors recalled interviews in which:

- Explaining that she hadn't eaten lunch, applicant wolfed down a burger and fries during interview.
- Applicant with receding hairline left the office and returned minutes later wearing a toupee.
- Applicant sat down with a Walkman clamped to her skull, explaining that she could listen to the interviewer and her favourite music at the same time.
- Applicant stopped the interview to phone his psychiatrist for advice on how to answer questions.
- Applicant dozed off and began to snore.

Still, a job interviewer can't always take things at face value. Never forget the experience of the editor of a Nevada newspaper who looked up from his desk one day to see a stranger, covered with dust, a filthy hat on his head and a bedroll on his back. Flopping in a chair, the stranger muttered, "My starboard leg seems to be unshipped. I'd like about a hundred yards of line. I think I am falling to pieces. My name is Clemens and I've come to write for the paper." On a hunch, the editor hired him.

Good hunch. The young stranger was Samuel Clemens, soon to give birth to a couple of immortal rascals named Tom Sawyer and Huckleberry Finn.

The Only Good Lawyer . . .

The first thing we do, let's kill all the lawyers.

WILLIAM SHAKESPEARE PENNED THOSE WORDS for a minor character in his play *Henry VI* nearly four hundred years ago. Last month in a souvenir shop in Stratford, Ontario, I saw racks and racks of T-shirts, all sizes, all colours, all bearing the same slogan. "How are the lawyer T-shirts selling?" I asked the clerk.

"Can't keep 'em in stock," she replied with a smirk.

Ah, yes . . . lawyerphobia. The profession everybody loves to loathe. 'Twas ever thus.

Almost ever, anyway. The ancient Romans groused and grumbled about lawyers. The Bible smites them hip and thigh (Luke 11:46). The English poet Keats wrote, "I think we may class the lawyer in the natural history of monsters." The nation of Andorra was so unimpressed with lawyers that it banned them from its courtrooms by government decree way back in 1864. That decree is still in effect.

The twentieth century has been no kinder to the legal profession. Maybe it was the spectacle of sleaze-exuding courtroom carrion eaters like Melvin Belli and Marvin Mitchelson. Maybe it was the numbing realization that most of our politicians started out as lawyers. (Is that a lateral career move, or a demotion?) Lawyers have become society's official professional scapegoats, eclipsing even dentists and journalists.

How do I know? From all the lawyer jokes going around, that's how. Have you heard them?

What's brown and black and looks good on a lawyer?
— A doberman.

Why do piranhas refuse to attack lawyers?
— Professional courtesy.

What's the difference between a dead skunk and a
dead lawyer in the middle of the road?
— Skid marks in front of the skunk.

Why does Ottawa have the most lawyers and
Baie Comeau the most toxic waste dumps?
— Baie Comeau got first choice.

What do you call the fear lawyers experience
when they step in doggy-do?
— Fear of melting.

This is vicious stuff! So vicious that even some lawyers aren't laughing anymore. The American Bar Association is making nervous throat-clearing noises about "the dangers of lawyer-bashing."

So far the ABA hasn't threatened to sue anybody.

They'd have their attaché cases full if they did. A whole slew of anti-lawyer joke books has hit the bookstores. Titles such as *What to Do with a Dead Lawyer* and also one called *Skid Marks* (see joke above). There's a popular syndicated column in many Canadian newspapers called "Court Jesters." It's written by one Peter MacDonald and it's all about irregular court goings-on in this country — most of them hilarious, very few of them edifying to the lawyers involved.

Mr. MacDonald comes by his material first-hand. He's a practising lawyer in Hanover, Ontario.

That brings up a truly curious characteristic about the epidemic of lawyer jokes going around: most of the jokes come from lawyers.

Which may be the most promising feature of the profession — that its members have the grace to laugh at themselves.

One final lawyer joke. This one is about F. E. Smith, a brilliant turn-of-the-century British barrister with a tongue like a samurai's sword. Nobody, not even judges, cared to bandy words with F. E. Smith. He always won.

Well, almost always. Once, twitting a judge about the size of his belly, Smith asked if he expected a boy or a girl. "If it's a boy," said the judge, "I'll call him John. If it's a girl, I'll call her Mary. But if, as I suspect, it's only wind, I'll call it F. E. Smith."

Is Stupidity a Felony?

If poverty is the mother of crime,
stupidity is its father.

A FRENCH SATIRIST BY THE NAME of Jean de La Bruyère penned those words more than three hundred years ago, but they might have been lifted from yesterday's blotter at any police station in this country. A lot of things have changed in the past three centuries but not, I submit, the amount of grey matter between the ears of your average sneakthief, snatchpurse, or cutthroat. They're still stupid after all these years.

There are degrees of dumb, however. The heistmeister who hit the Bank of Commerce in Cambridge, Ontario, a while back broke a cardinal bank-robbing commandment — he left his face hanging out for bystanders to see and remember. But at least he did it in style. The guy showed up at the teller's wicket decked out in a three-piece suit and sunglasses with an expensive-looking attaché case dangling from his well-manicured mitt. He passed the teller an I-have-a-bomb-in-my-briefcase note, scooped several thousand dollars into his briefcase, and left.

In a chauffeur-driven white limousine.

It was a rental from a nearby town. The crook had told the driver he wanted to "look at some real estate" in the area.

"He put up a big cash deposit for the rental," said the limo driver.

Not as big as his cash withdrawal, I bet.

In the never-ending turf war between cops and robbers it's not always the bad guys who show idiocy above and beyond the call. Consider the red-faced officers of Halton County, in southern Ontario, who recently lost a dangerous prisoner. They were driving said prisoner between jails in a prison van. When they got to their destination, they went around to the back of the truck and found the door bent open and the prisoner long gone. "Didn't you hear anything?" the desk sergeant wanted to know. Well, actually, no. The two guards had this killer rock-and-roll tape on the van's four-speaker stereo, y'see, and . . .

The Halton Board of Police has since voted to ban pleasure radios in prisoner escort vans.

Once in a very long while you encounter a crook who transcends the usual boundaries of mere stupidity and vaults into a whole new category of clod-dom so breathtaking it doesn't even have a name yet.

Let's call it hyperstunned.

Such a candidate is the chap currently staying at a Crowbar Hotel in North Carolina. It all started one sunny Saturday morning, the kind of morning where you get up and say, "Boy, what a great day to cut the lawn!" No such luck for our anti-hero. First, he lost control of his vehicle and ploughed into a truck. Two other cars ran into each other trying to avoid the crash. Police arrived, handcuffed our man, and popped him into the front seat of their police cruiser while they took statements from the other drivers. Next thing they saw was their patrol car disappearing down the highway. After abandoning the car, our man (handcuffed, mind) led police on a half-hour footrace before they finally brought him down, hauled him off to the slammer, and threw the book at him. His charges are various: driving while impaired, driving while his licence was revoked, improper registration, larceny, hit and run causing personal injury, careless driving, and reckless driving.

Not a laughing matter, to be sure . . . until you find out that the first vehicle our man was piloting was *a lawnmower.*

Pretty dumb, but not all-time dumb. That honour goes to Willie J. Collins, who stormed into an Atlanta police station not long ago and indignantly showed the desk sergeant the very bad quality cocaine some . . . *thief* had sold him.

Mr. Collins is in jail, but not forgotten. He serves to remind us just why they call that stuff "dope."

The Earth Is **Flat,** *I Tell You!*

S O THESE FOUR BOISTEROUS GUYS, these . . . louts, in their cheap flashy suits and hair down over their collars, come roiling into this very posh penthouse office, which happens to belong to the marketing manager of EMI Records. They are laughing and wisecracking and generally behaving in a fashion obnoxious enough to get them turfed out of a dockside pub. Their chances of favourably impressing the assembled recording industry moguls must be deemed . . . remote.

God knows how they got past the receptionist. They have (of course) a demo tape that they know the record men are going to love. The marketing manager takes the tape, gives the vagabonds the old don't-call-us-we'll-call-you routine, and shows them to the door.

When the door hisses shut there are great rollings of eyes among the stogie-smoking executives lounging around the office. Kids these days. Honestly.

Ho hum. Another unmagical moment. The punk quartet might have been dazzling and attractive and captivating. They weren't. The record executives might have had an intuitive hunch about the kids. They didn't. The demo tape might have been a blazing work of undeniable genius. It wasn't. Three of the four top executive music producers at EMI did the marketing manager a favour by listening to it.

They all agreed that it stank.

And the fourth executive music producer? Well, he was on holiday.

So ends another nonchapter in the history of human evolution. For every great flowering of human endeavour, there must be an awful lot of seed that falls upon stony ground.

Think of the mouldering bones of all the sailors whose ships disappeared over the western horizon before Columbus went and came back, proving it could be done.

Think of the near-misses in history — the skipper of the PT boat 108; the unsung heroes of the Charge of the Heavy Brigade; the martyrs who gave their all to take the Bridge on the River Ken.

Spare a thought for our own Gordon Lightfoot and his perfectly good singles that never quite enjoyed the success his other records did. I'm thinking of hard-to-find numbers such as "Canadian Pathway Trilogy," "The Wreck of the Edmund Fitzpatrick," and "Black Day in Early April."

Spare a kind thought, too, for Dr. Dionysius Lardner. Dr. Lardner was (and I'm not making this up) a professor of natural philosophy and astronomy at University College in London during the early 1800s. He is primarily remembered for his exquisitely argued and eminently reasonable assertions that high-speed rail travel would always be impossible, as passengers, unable to breathe, would suffocate.

The doctor also pooh-poohed the possibility of any steamship ever crossing the Atlantic, since it would require more coal than it could carry.

Somewhat later, a scientist by the name of Simon Newcomb harrumphed to the press that the ages-old dream of heavier-than-air flying machines was just that — a dream. "Impractical and insignificant, if not utterly impossible."

Professor Newcomb made that pronouncement in 1901, about eighteen months before a pair of brothers named Wilbur and Orville made famous a place called Kitty Hawk.

Ah, yes, History in her perversity makes it easy for us to be spectacularly wrong.

Such as the schoolmaster who labelled little Tommy Edison retarded. Or the Munich schoolteacher who warned a ten-year-old student, "You will never amount to very much." A student named Albert Einstein.

Such as the musical tableau I mentioned back at the beginning. Well, the four louts were loutish all right, but they were also persistent. When they heard that three of the company's top music moguls hated their demo tape, they didn't slink away with their tails between their legs. They insisted on playing it for the fourth music producer — the one who'd been away on holidays.

A fellow named George Martin.

And that's how the Beatles got their first record contract.

Hot Enough fer Ya?

Everybody talks about the weather,
but nobody does anything about it.

EVERYBODY THINKS THAT Mark Twain wrote that, but he didn't. A pretty well utterly forgotten scribbler by the name of Charles Dudley Warner penned that observation way back in 1897 in an editorial that appeared in the *Hartford Courant*. Somehow, history bungled it, and now the whole world thinks the credit belongs to Mark Twain.

That doesn't surprise me. Weather is a treacherous topic best untrifled with.

But the hell with it. It's a blustery, cruddy late spring day; there's a pair of worm-lusting robins hunched over on my front lawn like a couple of winos on a street corner; there's a leak in my basement, a draft under the back door, my cat's got spring fever, which means I have to get up every three minutes and forty-five seconds to either let him out or let him in . . . and I feel like picking on somebody.

So let's beat up on . . . the weatherman.

You know what bugs me most about weathermen? Not that they're wrong all the time.

As a matter of fact, they're not. Their forecasts are reasonably accurate — at least as reliable as Old Man Maidle's down the road. He keeps track of squirrels' acorn stashes and the thickness of caterpillar pelts. He also has a whole bunch of agricultural rhymes about the weather. Rhymes like "Crick don't flow, watch fer snow," and "Cows in the clover, summer's 'bout over."

I figure Old Man Maidle's weather poetry is dead-accurate

about 50 percent of the time — which is about the same as the guy with the Magic Marker on TV.

No, it's not the weather forecasters' accuracy (or lack of it) that bothers me. It's how when they are wrong, they . . . *never apologize*.

It's true! They can tell you on Friday that Saturday's going to be a great day for a picnic, and you can go to the park with your little hamper of egg salad sandwiches and Thermos of Freshie and wind up clinging to a floating picnic table in a deluge that makes the Johnstown flood look like a sunshower. You get home that night and turn on your TV and does Mr. Blow-Dry Pompadour apologize for his goof? Nah. He smiles and banters about the Blue Jays with the Sports Jockette and points a well-manicured (dry!) finger towards the low-pressure trough over Baffin Island that is going to, he says, make Sunday a "great day for a picnic."

Once, just once, I'd like to see the weatherman pop up on my TV screen right after the newscast, all decked out in manacles and prison greys. I'd like to hear him confess incompetence for missing yesterday's blizzard, plead guilty to lousy forecasting in general, then commit the weatherpersons' equivalent of hara-kiri: falling on his telescopic pointer in front of the Canada Weather Map.

It won't happen in my lifetime, of course — but I would have settled for watching TV in Britain the night after the devastating hurricane of 1987.

This really happened, folks.

Following his newscast, the BBC news anchor turned to weatherman Ian McCaskill and said, on live TV, "Well, Ian, you chaps were a fat lot of good last night."

Ian defended himself meekly, pointing out that they had forecast a "rather windy, showery airflow."

"No kidding," responded the anchor witheringly. "If you can't forecast the worst storm for several centuries, what are you doing?"

Poor Ian McCaskill. He and all the other British weather forecasters really didn't have a leg to stand on — particularly when it was revealed that weathermen in France, Spain, and the Netherlands had forecast the hurricane, using data obtained from the weather centre in . . .

Reading, England.

If only Ian had double-checked with Old Man Maidle . . .

You Think You've Got Troubles?

Nobody know the trouble I've seen.

— old blues refrain

IT HAS NOT BEEN A GOOD WEEK so far, friends. For one thing, my trusty four-wheeled rustbucket has come down with an asthmatic and expensive-sounding rasp in its carburetored throat. Then there's that phone message from the bank asking me to call back ASAP. Plus the envelope from Revenue Canada that I've been shuffling to the bottom of the in-basket since last Thursday. And those shooting stars I see every time I bend over to tie my shoes . . .

Know what I like to do when my troubles start to pile up — besides writing a whiny column about it, I mean? I like to dig out a tome called *The Book of Failures* by Stephen Pile. It is subtitled "A Splendid Panorama of Non-Achievement" — and indeed it is. Chronicled on the pages of *The Book of Failures* are the non-quite-feats and close-but-no-Panatella attempts of dozens upon dozens of fellow schlemiels whose run of bad luck makes me feel like changing my name to Leif the Lucky.

Such as? Well, such as the members of a British scuba-diving club who decided to get themselves into the *Guinness Book of World Records* by taking the plunge into the most inaccessible body of water in the entire British Isles. Poring over maps, they found Scotland's remotest loch. They rented Land Rovers, Highland guides, and mountain-climbing gear. They drove 740 chassis-fracturing miles, clambered 7,000 feet up a mountainside. They found their loch, made camp, donned their scuba gear, took the icy plunge into the black, foreboding waters —

And discovered that the loch was four feet deep.

My other favourite piece of bad news comes not from *The Book of Failures* but from the pages of a recent newspaper. It concerns the shoplifting trial of Florence Powers of New Jersey. Ms. Powers's psychiatrist testified that his client should be found innocent because she was under stress at the time of the incidents, due to: a recent auto accident, a traffic ticket, a new car purchase, overwork, husband's kidney stones, husband's asthma, hot flashes, vaginal itch, a bad rash, fear of cancer, fear of dental surgery, son's asthma, mother's illness, aunt's illness, pressure of organizing parent's fiftieth wedding anniversary, need to cook Thanksgiving dinner for twenty relatives, purchase of two hundred gifts for Christmas and Hanukkah, stress of selling house without realtor, lawsuit against wallpaper cleaners, purchase of furniture that had to be returned, and a faulty toilet.

I don't know about you, but a litany of misery like that automatically makes me feel better.

Not Ms. Powers, though, I guess.

She's got one new woe to add to her list.

A shoplifting conviction.

Freeze! It's the Spud Police!

The twentieth century belongs to Canada.

SIR WILFRID LAURIER UTTERED that smug prediction, back at the turn of the last century. Sir Wilfrid was a tad premature. Here in the dying embers of the time period in question, one might argue that the twentieth century belonged to America, Russia, Europe, Japan — maybe even Korea, but not to the Great White North. The past ninety-odd years lavished many blessings and rewards upon Canucks, but not, I think, custodianship of the century.

Pity. Would have been so tidy, being able to tag a hundred years of turmoil as "The Canadian Century." Historians like to catalogue periods of time that way. Thus we have the Pleistocene epoch, the Edwardian era, and the iron age. Journalists are fond of subdividing it even further into decades: the Roaring Twenties, the Dirty Thirties, the Swinging Sixties, the Me Decade of the eighties.

I have no idea how the nineties will go down in the history books, but I have a modest suggestion for the year we're in.

How about the Year of the Veggie?

These are volatile times for vegetables. Take the potato. Take, in fact, the only province in the Dominion that is known around the world for its potatoes — P.E.I.

They don't call it Spud Island for nothing.

It's received scant attention in the press, but the fact is, your average Prince Edward Islander now faces criminal charges if he or she dares to grow potatoes in his or her vegetable garden.

The provincial government is trying to stomp out a virus, called PVYN, that likes to cohabit with potato plants. To that end, the government has created a brand-new law enforcement agency called the Prince Edward Island Potato Police. Officers of the PEIPP come armed with court orders, search warrants, and bulldozers to plough under bootleg potato patches. Lawbreakers who flout the will of the legislature and attempt to cultivate homegrown french fries face a fine of up to $25,000.

I *swear* I'm not making this up.

What makes this story exceptionally loony is that the PVYN virus is utterly harmless to humans and potatoes. Officials want to stomp out the virus because it is lethal to tobacco plants.

Which, of course, kill Canadians by the tens of thousands every year.

Would that the tubers of P.E.I. had a champion like Steven Acquafresca of Colorado. Earlier this year Mr. Acquafresca quarterbacked a bill through the Colorado senate that promised to "protect fruits and vegetables from slander." As an apple grower, Acquafresca was incensed over reports that the chemical Alar, sprayed on apple trees, could cause cancer. Apple sales plummeted, even though the Alar data turned out to be inconclusive. Mr. Acquafresca contended that law-abiding fruits and vegetables should be protected from such unsubstantiated rumours.

Unhappily for Acquafresca, his bill amounted to so much applesauce. It was hooted down by Colorado legislators, who complained that it would "prune the Constitution of the right of free speech" and "treat a lima like a human bean."

That's the trouble with being a fruit or vegetable — no respect.

Although now that I think of it, P.E.I. spuds do have one goodwill ambassador. This fella even wrote a song about them. One verse goes:

> *It's Bud the Spud, from the big red mud,*
> *Rollin' down the highway smilin'*
> *The spuds are big, on the back of Bud's rig,*
> *They're from Prince Edward Island.*

That Stompin' Tom — he sure knows his onions.

Stompin' Tom for Poet Laureate

How beautifully useless,
how deliciously defiant
a poem is!

— Raymond Souster

TELL THE TRUTH, now — when's the last time you picked up a book of poetry?

Yeah. Me too. I manage to wade through *Maclean's, Saturday Night*, the *Globe and Mail*, my local paper — even a novel or two each week. But poetry? Sorry, no time.

Part of the reason is of course that much modern poetry is so infuriatingly inaccessible. Here, for instance, is the last gasp of the final stanza of a Joe Rosenblatt poem:

BUZZZZZZZ
BUZZZZZZ
BUZZZZZ
BUZZZZ
BUZZ
BUZ
ZZ

That may be tremendously meaningful to Joe Rosenblatt. It may even be kinda fun to watch him "perform" it at, say, the Hamilton Steelworkers Annual Christmas Party.

But Shakespeare it ain't.

A lot of modern poetry seems to be little more than cerebral foreplay between the author and his or her consciousness. Too bad. As Robertson Davies says, "Poetry is undoubtedly a serious business . . . but the world also needs its entertainers, its bards, who remind us that poetry was not always a question of printed pages, hidden meanings, and dismal intellectual gropings; there was a time when poetry was for everybody, and had some fun in it."

I think Joseph Brodsky would second that. Mr. Brodsky is a Soviet émigré, kicked out of the U.S.S.R. twenty years ago because his poems infuriated the Politburo. Brodsky picked himself up, dusted himself off, and moved to the U.S. Eventually the Americans honoured him with the title of U.S. poet laureate.

Brodsky is an old-style poet. The kind who thinks poems ought to be read by everyone, not just weedy academics and neo-Beatnik wannabes.

And he just might do something about it. Brodsky told a Washington audience recently that poetry ought to be sold in supermarkets and left in every motel room, right next to the Gideon Bible. "The Bible won't mind this," he explained. "It doesn't mind being next to the telephone book."

He'd also like to see racks of poetry books available at the corner drugstore. "Poems are cheaper than tranquillizers, and reading them may reduce the bill from your shrink." Rising to the moment, Brodsky declared, "Poetry is perhaps the only insurance we've got against the vulgarity of the human heart, and it should be available to everyone at low cost."

Well, it's not an entirely original thought. One of our own poets, Irving Layton, once wrote, "If the walls that separate people from people are ever pulled down, it will not be done by politicians or dictators. It will be done by poets."

I don't think it would hurt if we broadened our definition of "poet" either. Bruce Cockburn is a Canadian poet. So are k. d. lang, Gordon Lightfoot, Rita MacNeil . . . and Wayne Gretzky.

That's not an original thought, either. One of Brodsky's ex-compatriots, Yevgeny Yevtushenko, once visited these shores and announced, "I say the best Canadian poet is Phil Esposito." Then he added thoughtfully, "And that is not a joke."

I say: Stompin' Tom Connors for Canadian poet laureate.

And I'm only joking a little bit.

Grunts from the Locker Room

W ELL THE REST OF YOU CAN HOOP and holler over who's gonna win the National League East or the American League West or the Kumquat League South or whatever. I don't care that baseball's winding down, football's heating up, and hockey's facing off. For me, the sports story of the year has already come and gone. Happened in a football locker room not long ago where a party of naked gorillas who normally appear in New England Patriot football uniforms exposed themselves and said some very naughty words to Boston *Herald* reporter Lisa Olsen. Did they take this measure because they didn't like Lisa Olsen's reportage? No, they did it because Lisa Olsen is a woman and she was in their tree fort — errr, dressing room.

I love it. This is the kind of the thing that helps to jolt the sports world back into perspective — which is a venue it hasn't played for quite some time. Sports used to be fun. A diversion, a pastime. But then it turned solemn.

Writers started scrivening elegies and litanies about Super Bowls and World Series and Stanley Cups as if they were somehow more significant than mere mortal life. Young bulgy fellers with greater than average hand-eye coordination and not much else signed contracts, moved out of the cane fields and hay mows and into downtown penthouses, with limos at the curb and Playboy centrefolds on their arms. Suddenly sport wasn't sport anymore. It was Little Boy Nirvana, with good guys and bad guys, where winning was heaven and losing is hell. Sure, *hell.* Why do you think they call overtime "sudden death"?

The truth about professional sport is somewhat less edifying. "Serious sport," said George Orwell, "has nothing to do with fair play. It is bound up with hatred, jealousy, boastfulness, disregard of all rules and sadistic pleasure in witnessing violence . . . it is war, minus the shooting."

Often performed, Orwell might have added, by men minus the grey matter — as witness the baboons in the Patriot locker room.

But that said, you would have to wonder what kind of a reporter, male, female, or androgynous, needs to be in a room full of sweaty jocks hosing down after a grunt-fest. I mean, how would you feel if you hopped out of your shower to find Clark Kent or Lois Lane perched on your toilet holding out a microphone and saying, "Arthur, you came up flat out there today. Do you think this might be your final season?"

It's fairly normal not to enjoy bantering with fully dressed strangers while clad in a towel. Happens to the best of us. Even Winston Churchill. Back in the twenties, Churchill gave Nancy Astor, the first woman to take a seat in the British House of Commons, a pretty hard time. When she asked him why, Churchill explained that he found her presence in the all-male House embarrassing — as embarrassing, he said, as if she had burst into his bathroom when he had nothing on. Lady Astor eyed the dumpy Churchill up and down disdainfully and replied, "Winston, you're not nearly attractive enough to have worries of that kind."

Pity Nancy's not around to take a post-game scrum in the Patriot locker room. She'd be all over those jock jerks like an L.A. Raider blitz.

Of Hogs and Hiccups

S O HOW'S IT GOIN'? Pretty bleh, eh? Same old stuff? Get up get dressed get fed go to work come home check the mail fall asleep during "The Journal" go to bed get up and do it all over again tomorrow?

That how it is for you? Feeling a little bored, are you? Like your groove has turned into a rut?

Well, cheer up. Things could be a lot worse. You could be Charlie Osborne.

Charlie was a guy who had a pretty good life. Successful hog farmer down in Anthon, Iowa. Respect of his colleagues, affection from his friends, credit at the bank. But Charlie had that itch. He wanted something more.

Which is maybe why you'd find him doing . . . odd things. Things that normal, happy, well-adjusted people probably wouldn't think of doing. Things like, well, picking up swine, for instance. Charlie would go around picking up porkers in his arms, just for the fun of it.

It started out harmlessly enough — a suckling here, a barrow there, maybe on a Saturday night the odd gilt or a shoat. But it got to be a *thing* with Charlie. Pretty soon he was hoisting young sows and immature boars . . . and they were getting bigger and bigger. Understand, we're talking uncooperative, wriggling pig meat here. It's not just the dead weight, it's the live hog.

It was on a cool autumn afternoon that Charlie Osborne met his weiner Waterloo. He wrestled down, bear-hugged, and hoisted a 218-pound hog right off the ground. When he put it back down, Charlie opened his mouth to say something. And what he said was *hic*!

Charlie's been making that same monosyllabic comment ever since. Sometimes Charlie Osborne has been saying *hic* at a rate of forty times a minute. Other times it subsides to once every mere ten or fifteen seconds. But Charlie never stops hiccupping — or at least he hasn't so far.

Oh, it's caused problems. Charlie doesn't sleep real well, as you can imagine. Hard for him to eat, too . . . he takes most of his meals through a blender. Charlie says it's tough even to keep false teeth in: his hiccups are irregular, bushwhacky and powerful, which tends to blow his choppers clear across the kitchen.

But there's good news. Charlie's fathered five kids, and not a hiccupper among them. The other good news is that . . . Charlie survived. That first *hic* bubbled up Charlie's esophagus back in 1922. He's now pushing the century mark. And still hiccupping.

So next time the bills start lapping at your tibia and you think your kid's rap CD is going to drive you insane and the car kind of flutters and warbles when you hit the gas and the boss is giving you that dead mackerel stare again . . . just stop and ask yourself this: If all your troubles were rolled into one ball, would it be bigger or smaller than the prospect of living more than seven decades without ever enjoying *one minute* of not hiccupping — like Charlie Osborne? Sure. Count your blessings.

And just to be on the safe side, you come across any 218-pound hogs, just leave 'em right where you found 'em. Charlie Osborne would.

TV Westerns: Telling It like It Wasn't

I 'VE SEEN A LOT of cultural weirdness in my time, everything from Andy Warhol's soup can paintings through the sack dress and all the way to Stompin' Tom Connors. But I think one of the very oddest fads I ever sat through was the TV western.

Remember TV westerns? If you grew up in the fifties and sixties, you couldn't get away from them. Every evening after the dishes were washed and stacked, television sets across the continent blazed to life as all of North America gathered around their cathode campfires to absorb a little more western lore as dispensed by Hollywood. Westerns bushwacked the TV airwaves every evening and held us all for ransom — or at least till the eleven-o'clock news.

How many westerns were there? Who could count them all? I have a trivia book that lists eighty-nine western TV series — and I can think of a couple that aren't mentioned. But for anyone who's too young to remember, or who spent their youth picking ticks off yaks in a Tibetan lamasery, here's a brutally truncated shortlist:

"Lancer." "Laramie." "Laredo." "The Lawman." "The Legend of Jesse James." "The Life and Legend of Wyatt Earp." "Lone Ranger." "The Loner."

And those, my friends, are just the westerns that began with *L*.

The cowboys immortalized in celluloid had a variety of occupations as wide as the Texas panhandle. Matt Dillon was a marshal;

Brett Maverick was a cardsharp. Ward Bond rode herd on a wagon train, while Lucas McCain ("The Rifleman") was a jut-jawed single-parent farmer, trying to raise his young lad in between bouts of blowing away baddies with his modified Winchester lever action. There were wandering confederate soldiers ("The Rebel") and Shakespeare-spouting hit men ("Paladin"); good guys who often took guitar breaks (Gene Autry) and bizarre guys who foiled Colt .45s with Oriental mumbles closely followed by lightning kicks to the earhole ("Kung Fu").

The TV westerns had a couple of things in common. For one thing, approximately 6.5 humans bit the dust per half-hour episode. And for another thing, very little real work ever seemed to get done.

But none of that bothered the fans. We sat and we watched, entranced, by the tens of millions. After all, TV westerns were our only pipeline to that most fabled era of North American history — the Wild West.

The ironic thing is, the Wild West was a hoax. A fraud. It never happened. At least, it never happened the way our history books — and the TV westerns — tell us it happened.

You would think from watching television that the era of the Wild West must have stretched out at least a century and a half. How could you cram all those hair-raising adventures into any less time? In fact, cowboys as working-class heroes had only about thirty good years, beginning right after the Civil War, when a cattle boom in Texas coincided with a lot of demobbed soldiers with nothing better to do than play nursemaid to herds of longhorns. Most cowboys were dirt-poor, none to bright, and teetering on the edge of malnutrition from a lousy diet of coffee, beans, and sourdough. Almost none of them wore guns — they couldn't afford to. They worked long, hard hours for next to nothing. Some of them spent so much time in the saddle they literally couldn't walk properly.

Another failing of the TV western: colour-blindness. Can you remember any TV westerns that featured a black cowboy hero? Or black cowboys at all? Wasn't much black in those black-and-white shows. Exceedingly odd, considering that one of every three cowboys working the range was black.

Ironically, there was one larger-than-life black cowboy. His name was John Ware. He rode like Kit Carson, shot like Bat Masterson, hunted like Daniel Boone, and ranched like Jim Redigo on "Empire."

Alas, John Ware had the misfortune to do all this on the banks of the Red Deer River in Alberta.

They don't make TV westerns there.

Smack! Right in the Kisser

A young woman and a young man had better not be alone together very much until they are married. This will be found to prevent a good many troubles. Kisses and caresses . . . have a direct and powerful physiological effect. Nay, they often lead to the most fatal results.

— from *A Complete Sexual Science and a Guide to Purity and Physical Manhood* (1894)

I REMEMBER WHEN I FIRST DID IT. Judy Page was her name. It was at my sister's wedding and I (rogue that I was) took advantage of all the nuptial confusion. I dragged Judy behind a curtain and we did it.

Just once. I was a beginner, after all.

Not like Paul and Sadie Andover, two passionate Americans who hold the world record: 20,009 times in two hours.

Not like the three couples sprawled in the parking lot of a furniture shop in Reno, Nevada, recently. Tourists and shoppers practically had to climb over them as they did it *tout ensemble* right there on the main drag!

What's that, madame? You say you're faxing a petition to the justice minister to have me drawn and quartered in the shade of the Peace Tower? Relax.

It's *osculation* we're talking about here. Paul and Sadie Andover *kissed* each other 20,009 times in two hours. Those three Reno couples in the parking lot were joined only at the lips.

As for Judy and me, well, what do you expect? She was the flower girl and I was the page boy. We couldn't have made one teenager even if you added our ages together!

Judy and I did it out of curiosity, I guess. Paul and Sadie did it to get their names in the record book. The Reno Sextet did it strictly for money. They were contestants in an event called the Great American Kiss-Off, a promotion sponsored by a Nevada furniture store that offered $10,000 U.S. to the couple that could kiss the longest. Contestants had to smooch for twelve hours each day, from nine in the morning till nine at night, right out there in the furniture store's parking lot. They got a five-minute break each hour to reapply their lipstick and water the flowers — otherwise it was nose-to-nose with their loved one from dawn to dusk.

How long do you think you could buss your sweetie under those conditions? Half a day? Three days? A week?

The Nevada Nuzzlers held out — and on — for *forty-two days*. In fact, they'd probably still be nibbling at each other except the furniture company got tired of not having a parking lot. Company officials awarded the ten grand to all six contestants and let them split it up any way they liked.

Strange way to say hello, though — kissing. When I was a kid we used to laugh about the Eskimos and their habit of rubbing noses. But is that any more bizarre than our custom of planting juicy smackers on one another's lips? I wouldn't want to argue it in a court of law.

Which is where some kissers ended up, by the way. Like the twenty-four-year-old Oklahoman who was convicted of assault back in 1976 and fined $200. His crime? Kissing the elbow — the elbow! — of a parking warden while she was giving him a ticket.

Things were even tougher in England during the early 1800s. Any chap caught kissing his wife on a Sunday could expect to spend two hours in the stocks.

All of which brings to mind a morsel of doggerel that's been dancing around in my head ever since I read about the Great American Kiss-Off:

> *She frowned and called him Mr.*
> *Because in sport he kr.*
> *And so in spite*
> *That very nite*
> *This Mr. kr. sr.*

Don't know a thing about the poet, but I'll bet you a french kiss he wasn't a nineteenth-century Englishman.

How Much Ya Wanna Bet?

So YOU THINK YOU GOT what it takes to be a professional gambler, eh, pal? Well, let me give you two pieces of gambling advice. Number one: In pressure games, always bet against the Dallas Cowboys, the Detroit Tigers, and Germany.

That's a tip I got from a gambler. I don't know if it works, but I've been waiting for a chance to say it for years.

My second piece of advice comes from a Damon Runyon story. It's a gambler dad passing along some advice to his would-be gambler son. "Son," he says, "as you go around and about in this world, some day you will come upon a man who will lay down in front of you a new deck of cards with the seal unbroken, and offer to bet he can make the jack of spades jump out of the deck and squirt cider in your ear.

"Son," the old man continued, "do not bet him, because as sure as you do, you are going to get an earful of cider."

Okay, you've all heard the disclaimer; everybody's read the warning on the package that says gambling can lead to acute poverty. Now let's have some fun with barroom bets. See this perfectly average paperclip I've got in my hand? Ten bucks says you can't guess, to the nearest half inch, how long it'll be when I straighten it out. Whaddaya figure — inch and a half? Two inches? Two and a half? Nope. Time's up. The answer if four inches, and if you don't believe me wreck a normal paperclip and find out. Oh yeah . . . and you owe me ten bucks.

Little green at barroom bets, are you? Well, don't feel bad, so was Mark Anthony. He really got hustled by Cleopatra. She bet him that she could drink half a million dollars' worth of wine without getting up from the table. The aptly named "Mark" said, "You're on, Cleo." Whereupon Cleopatra pinched two near-priceless pearls from a string around her neck, popped them in her goblet, and chuggalugged to win the bet.

Gotta be careful of barroom bets. They thrive on suckers. And suckers can be on either side of the pot. Like the guy who went into the bar with a parrot on his shoulder and announced loudly, "This parrot can sing 'The Little Drummer Boy' and do all the parts — from the drum riff to the last soprano in the Harry Simeon Chorale. Anybody want to bet I'm wrong?" Bartender looks at him, says, "Okay, pal, I'll take your money." Lays fifty on the bar. Couple other guys along the bar have been listening, they move over and add their money. Pretty soon the bar is carpeted with cash. Parrot owner can barely cover the bets, but he does, then turns to the bird. "Pretty Polly. Polly sing. Little Drummer Boy. Prrrrump pah. Go ahead."

Nothin'. The bird might as well be the Maltese Falcon. The guy is cleaned out. Walking home, he says to the parrot, "What's the matter with you? You humiliated me. You cost me my last dime. Why didn't you sing?"

Parrot says, "Get serious. Think how high the odds are gonna be when we go back in there next week."

Ah, yes. Gambling. Another famous Mark — with the last name Twain — said: "There are two times in a man's life when he should not speculate. When he can't afford it and when he can." Ah, good old Twain. Born in Florida, you know. Was so! Betcha ten bucks.

You lose. Mark Twain (or Samuel Clemens) was born in 1835 in the tiny town of Florida, Missouri.

That's twenty bucks you owe me, pal.

And could you rebend those paperclips before you leave?

Gambling: You Got a Lotto Lose

The lottery: a tax on fools.

— Henry Fielding

SOMETIMES A PICTURE REALLY IS worth a thousand words. A few weeks ago the newspapers carried a photograph that said more about the idiocy of lotteries than a hundred-page manifesto from Gamblers Anonymous.

The photo showed a guy lying on the hood of his car, which was parked in front of a Florida convenience store. He was staying there all night so that he could be first in line when the store opened in the morning. He intended, the photo caption said, to spend his last $800 on lottery tickets.

It was part of the latest outbreak of lottomania that occurred in Florida recently. The top prize in the state lottery was worth over $100 million, and suddenly people were buying ten, fifteen tickets at a time. Some hopefuls spent their rent money. Others arranged bank loans.

Just think of the sub-human level of logic. Some of these folks wouldn't have bothered to buy a ticket if the prize had been, say, $100,000. But $100 million? Florida looked like a shark feeding frenzy. Despite the fact that every ticket sold increased the odds against winning, the lineups of hopefuls stretched for blocks.

It's a strange addiction, lottomania. Some people live for their weekly fix. I know a lady who lays out twenty bucks every Thursday morning at the corner store. All Thursday afternoon she's as high as gyrfalcon, humming Broadway tunes and chattering about faraway places.

Then comes Friday morning. She's lost again and she's down in the dumps. Which is where she stays until another Thursday morning rolls around.

I figure she's happy for about six hours a week. Heck, most drugs give a better return than that. I've thought of telling her that I know an easy way she could save a thousand dollars a year, but a little voice tells me she doesn't want to hear it. Lottomaniacs do love their vice.

Even though it can kill them. Bill Curry, a thirty-seven-year-old Boston cafeteria worker, won $4 million and change in the Massachusetts lottery not long ago. He died of a heart attack two weeks later. His sister-in-law said Curry's health began to go downhill the day he found out he'd won. He was hounded by old acquaintances who suddenly became best friends, by self-appointed financial advisers, and by strangers seeking money for everything from major surgery to Madagascar tin mines.

"It was the stress of it that killed him," says the sister-in-law.

That's the trouble with easy money: in the long run, it's not that easy.

Pauline Glassman knew that. She's a Toronto woman who, several years ago, was a bag lady, sleeping in parks and eating out of restaurant dumpsters, wandering through the alleys and laneways of downtown Toronto. In 1982 she disappeared and was given up for dead. Then, just recently, a private detective found her alive and married, on welfare, in a tiny apartment in a subsidized housing project in Toronto.

At first she denied being Pauline Glassman, but the detective had done his homework. As well he might. The detective was being well paid by a large trust company that urgently wanted to find Pauline Glassman.

To tell her that, due to an inheritance, she was now a millionaire.

But the best part is — Pauline Glassman didn't want the money! She said that the past five years with her new husband had been "the best years of my life" — so wonderful that not only did the prospect of wealth not tempt her but she feared it might ruin all the joy she'd found.

Smart lady. Alas, smooth talkers in charge of the estate convinced her otherwise. Pauline Glassman gave in and is now a rich woman.

I guess all we can do is wish her good luck.

I'll Sue You in My Dreams

BUDDY, CAN YOU SPARE A DIME? Chances are you can't. Times are tough and money's tight. Nevertheless, there are still some ways to generate cash in these lean mean days. For instance, have you considered mounting a lawsuit?

There's a cash cow for you — and you don't have to be hit by a truck, fired by a chauvinist, or poisoned by a fast-food burger to sue, you know. Heck, no. I mean, you're probably better off than Richard Kreimer — and he sued his entire home town, Morristown, New Jersey. Kreimer's a street person. Doesn't shave, doesn't bathe. Changes his clothes about once a season. Kreimer looks bad and smells worse. Predictably, he gets rousted from public places such as restaurants, laundromats, and the Morristown library with fair regularity. But Kreimer is a scrapper. He sued the town for harassment. Last month he was awarded $150,000 U.S. for his suffering.

Not that we Canucks need any lessons from the Yanks when it comes to filing lawsuits. One particularly grim December evening, Lakeheader Gregory Daragavel got juiced up, stole a snowplough, and started rearranging some parked cars in downtown Thunder Bay. Greg went to jail for a year and now he's out. And suing the Thunder Bay police force for not arresting him for drunkenness before he went on his rampage.

Not quite frivolous enough for you? How about the case of Eric Graham? He's suing for $10,000 in damages from a Florida mall barbershop. His grievance? Bad haircut. Eric says the clip he got was too short on top and too long on the sides. So much so that he has been forced to wear a hat and seek psychiatric help.

Then there's the guy in Alberta who is suing the Alberta Fish and Game Association because they won't let him hunt. The fish and fur folks assumed that Herman Biffert should be kept away from guns — because he is stone-blind. Mr. Biffert scoffs at that. "I go hunting with my son," he says. "I don't carry the gun until we line up on an animal. When he's got the animal focused in the scope, he says 'pull the trigger,' and that's what I do." Well, it's not exactly the "Song of Hiawatha," Mr. Biffert, but I guess it beats shooting fish in a barrel.

And it's not quite as ambitious as the case of Boca Raton resident Charlie Moore. Charlie lost one eye in a hunting accident a couple of years ago, but he hasn't let his visual handicap interfere with the finer things in life — like going to the movies. Charlie loves the movies. He loves them so much that he feels ripped off. Which is why Charlie's suing the Boca Raton movie theatre. For a 50 percent movie theatre discount. Because Charlie, with his one eye, really only sees 50 percent of the screen action, right?

Let me leave you with my nomination for lawsuit of the decade. It concerns a British attorney by the name of Brian Fagumo, who is suing for slander. Who's he suing for slander? Not who — what. Mr. Fagumo has filed suit against . . . his talking bathroom scale. During a party, Mr. Fagumo stepped on his scale in the presence of some business colleagues. The next thing he and his friends heard was a tinny, mechanical voice saying "LOSE SOME WEIGHT, FATSO." Mr. Fagumo thinks a cheque for £50,000 from the makers of the bathroom scale would assist him in overcoming the shame and embarrassment the incident caused him.

How'd it turn out? I don't know.

No doubt we'll hear about it eventually on that CBC Radio program, "The Scales of Justice."

PART 3

Do We Really Need This Stuff?

Revenge at Last

THERE ARE TWO THINGS I will always love about Elvis Presley. One is the way he sang "That's All Right, Mama." The other is the way he shot up television sets.

Story goes that whenever Elvis played Vegas, there was an unspoken understanding with the hotel management that the King might need a new TV on very short notice. In fact, it wasn't inconceivable that he might require two or even three new ones sent up to his suite in a single night. That's because when it came to channel changing, Elvis was ahead of his time. If he was watching TV and somebody came on that he didn't like, ol' Elvis would haul out a gold-plated Colt .45, squint down the barrel, and dust that program — and the TV tube — straight into vacuumland. Legend has it that the TV icon Elvis most enjoyed blowing away was Robert Goulet, but that's probably too delicious to be true.

I can't count the number of times I've wanted to shoot my television — or at least put a Greb Kodiak through the screen. I never do it, of course. You have to be rich or psychopathic to get away with that.

Towards the end there, Elvis kind of had both bases covered.

My TV isn't the only hunk of hardware that fuels my homicidal fantasies. I've often dreamt of drop-kicking my Ronson electric, cuffing my clock radio, and slap-shooting my bedside alarm clock right out the bedroom window. My eight-foot Amana side-by-side is too massive for a simple, unarmed frontal assault, but that doesn't stop me from entertaining reveries of dropping a burning tractor tire over its top and necklacing the mother into the big display room in the sky.

What characteristic do all of the aforementioned chunks of technology share? Treachery. They have all, at one time or another, betrayed me. Usually when I needed them most. Not being rich — or owning a gold-plated Colt .45 — I have forgiven, but not forgotten.

But I've got a hunch the day of reckoning is at hand. In Atlanta, Georgia, there is a place called the Bullet Stop. It's a shooting range where you are the hunter and the quarry is — well, your sock-eating washing machine, maybe. Or perhaps that stupid toaster that skims burnt crusts across your kitchen like a skeet shoot. At Bullet Stop you can rent shotguns, handguns, semi- and full automatics, and then proceed to riddle the utility of your choice. And some of them are tougher than they look. One disgruntled housewife lit into her vacuum cleaner with a Thompson submachine gun. It absorbed fifty rounds before it finally hoovered its last.

Is mankind about to overthrow the technological tyrant? Recently some Pasadena, California, neighbours threw the world's first Sledge-O-Matic party. Participants gathered up all the machines in their lives that either didn't work or performed perversely, put them in a big pile — and then kicked hell out of them. Balky gizmos that breathed their last at this year's Sledge-O-Matic included a self-winding wristwatch that didn't, a cassette player still nonfunctional after nine cord replacements, and a colour TV that went on the fritz during the NCAA Final Four basketball playoffs. Where are these aberrant appliances now?

Ground to techno-rubble, every one.

Frankly, I like the concept — and I approve of Bullet Stop too. So would Ned Ludd. Ned was a splendid anarchist who led a band of merry pranksters through the north of England in the early 1800s, smashing textile machines wherever they found them. The Luddites lost the battle, of course. The Industrial Revolution swallowed us all, and sometimes, when I'm sitting in a car that won't start, or standing in an elevator that won't elevate, or contemplating the grey, blank stare of a computer monitor that's just eaten my newspaper column, I dream of throwing my own Sledge-O-Matic party and inviting Ned and his gang.

It would be a grand bash. We'd have music.

Elvis, of course.

On a hand-cranked Victrola.

Adopt-a-Ditch

I THINK IT'S THE STYROFOAM pop cooler that depresses me most. It's there every morning when I take my dog for a walk, poking the shards of its grey white bulk out of the ditch that runs beside the road I take. If it wasn't for the pop cooler, the scene would be worthy of a Robert Bateman landscape — a grove of gnarled cedars fanning out left and right, the black and ancient Grand River snaking through the background, a squadron of Canada geese in a low-level flypast looking for a likely corn field. I don't know how long the busted-up Styrofoam cooler has been lodged in the ditch — maybe years. Long enough to endure more than a few rains and snows without budging. Long enough to snag dozens of wrappers and plastic bags and other twentieth-century flotsam and jetsam that people throw over their shoulders or out their car windows without a second thought.

Every time I walk past the remains of that cooler I think to myself, what manner of brain-dead bozo would drive down this back road, see these trees, that river, those Canadas, and say to him- or herself, "Wow! What a perfect place to get rid of that old Styrofoam pop cooler!"

Somebody did. And not just a pop cooler, either. I don't have to squint to see the other crap we passersby have consigned to the ditch: beer bottles, pop cans, cigarette wrappers, Big Mac containers, Dunkin' Donuts bags.

As a species, we really are a pack of slobs.

Well, not all of us. There are people like Gordon Carle.

Mr. Carle is a commercial fisherman living on the outskirts of La Ronge, in northern Saskatchewan. Driving in to town one day, looking out his side window at several years' accumulated trash in the ditch, Mr. Carle cursed to himself and muttered something along the lines of "What a sight! Somebody should do something about that mess."

Which is when it dawned on Mr. Carle that he was driving alone, hence he was talking to himself.

If "somebody" was going to do something about that mess, it might as well be him.

But even in a relatively unspoiled spot like La Ronge, the ditches are too much for one man to handle. Carle decided to go for help. In his own frontier way. He didn't ask for government money. He didn't bug the Rotarians or the Kiwanis or the Lions. He just approached all the people he knew in the community and said, "Whaddaya say we adopt a ditch?"

The La Ronge Adopt-A-Ditch program was born. "We asked local people to volunteer to clean up just one kilometre of ditch, both sides," says Carle, "and we asked them to make a commitment to do it four times over the summer."

The idea took off. A La Ronge radio station supported the plan. Nearby communities jumped on the bandwagon. Mayors, downtown merchants, whole families, and members of a nearby native reserve jumped on the bandwagon. By summer's end, three hundred community volunteers had plucked the junk from more than 55 miles of ditches around La Ronge.

Next spring, Carle and company plan to tackle the junk that has collected for most of this century around the area's lakes and canoe routes — in addition to keeping the ditches clean.

We don't have a lot of lakes and canoe routes where I live, but we have a ton of dirty ditches. Bet you do too.

Think about it the next time you go for a drive. Check out the number of old mattresses, beer cartons, pop bottles, and Pampers you pass in half a mile. Not too daunting, eh? Nothing half a dozen volunteers with a pickup couldn't handle in, say, one Saturday afternoon in spring?

Why not start your own Adopt-a-Ditch program? It's not patented. You willing? I am.

But not this afternoon. This afternoon I have to go out and pick up a Styrofoam pop cooler.

Speak Up — I Can't Hear You

HERE'S A WONDERFUL new offering from twentieth-century science and technology — not to mention a sobering sign of the times. It's a wee gizmo about the size of an old-fashioned chamber pot called the Sleep Sound Generator. "This unique device" — I'm reading the flyer here — "produces a gentle whooshing noise that helps block out annoying sounds such as traffic or construction . . . so that you can fall asleep easily."

The Sleep Sound Generator is available at select department stores for $44.95 U.S.

So it's come to this, gentle readers: we can't buy golden silence anymore, so how about some nickel-plated noise? Not quite as annoying as the noise that's keeping you awake. You're still disturbed, but by a higher class of sound. Sort of like combatting B.O. by drenching yourself in cheap cologne rather than taking a bath. The Sleep Sound Generator offers anti-noise, as it were.

Perverse as it is, there must be a need for it. The world is getting louder. I used to complain whenever I got a hotel room with windows that didn't open — until I got a hotel room with windows that did. Shrieking ambulances, blatting taxi horns, wailing police sirens, boozy bozos singing off-key Blue Jay anthems — I couldn't hear my television, much less get to sleep. Nowadays when I check into a city hotel I don't ask for openable windows. I ask for an extra pillow — to clamp over my head.

Funny how folks will get all snarly if somebody lights a cigarette in a public place, but they don't let out a peep about jackhammers,

97

tandem trucks, or low-flying aircraft that just as surely pollute their air space. Maybe they *are* complaining. Maybe we just can't hear them for the noise. But it makes you wonder. Must outboards, snowmobiles, chainsaws, lawnmowers, motorbikes, those infernal jet skis, and men's electric shavers — must they all be as loud as assault artillery? Just asking.

Of course, a lot of noise pollution is self-inflicted. Sportscar owners could, if they wished, insist on quieter acceleration. They don't wish. Audiences at megadecibel rock concerts are not driven there at bayonet point. They pay big bucks to have their innards turned to sonic jelly.

Fine for them. Not so fine for bystanders who suffer secondary noise pollution just as surely as bartenders and taxi drivers endure secondary cigarette smoke. So what about the quieter, if not silent, majority who don't take in that many Metallica concerts, wouldn't have a boom-box radio as a gift, and shy away from in-car stereos powerful enough to curl the windshield wipers? What are *we* supposed to do? Move to the Barren Lands? Crochet some earmuffs? Well, we could. Or we could make a little noise ourselves. As a friend of mine once said, "I don't get annoyed when my neighbour plays his stereo till two in the morning. As a matter of fact, I call him up at 4 a.m. to tell him how much I enjoyed it."

I Owe You One, Alex

Mr. Watson, come here. I want you.

THOSE SEVEN FATEFUL WORDS were uttered 117 years ago. Anyone in the vicinity of the young inventor who said them would have concluded he was nuts. After all, it was 1876 — no cars, no electric lights, no radios — and here was a man in broad daylight, all by himself, talking into some newfangled jumble of wires and machinery.

He wasn't mad. He was Alexander Graham Bell. And he had just transmitted intelligible words by telephone for the first time.

A momentous moment in the history of mankind. Still, I wonder what Bell would make of his invention if he could walk our planet today. I wonder how he'd react to the sight of phone booths on street corners. Or the fact that people routinely ring up Memphis, Melbourne, or Moscow. What would he have to say about telephone answering machines? Could he in his wildest dreams have imagined that one day an American president would talk by phone with an astronaut orbiting the Moon?

Personally, I'd surrender my Bell Calling Card for the chance to see Alex's face as he listened in on a radio phone-in show.

The telephone has transformed all our lives just as surely — and perhaps as profoundly — as fire, the wheel, and Mr. Edison's wee, incandescent glass bulb.

But let's face it, it hasn't been roses all the way.

The miracle of the telephone also ushered in the curse of the obscene call, wrong numbers, heart-shattering intrusions during lovemaking . . . and worse.

Exhibit A: the cellular car phone.

I resent government intrusion as much as the next civil libertarian, but if our defence minister was to send in his jackbooted Van Doos tomorrow to confiscate and blast to smithereens every car phone from Come-By-Chance to the Queen Charlottes, he wouldn't hear a peep of disapproval from me. Have you had the experience yet? Driving down the highway, you suddenly face an oncoming set of high-beams weaving and strobing from one side of the road to the other, homing in on you like an Exocet missile. Your knuckles whiten on the wheel as you pump the brake and look for a good stretch of shoulder to slew your car onto. All the while, your brain, on red alert, is riffling through the possibilities — drunk? escaping bank robber? kamikaze commuter? Driving School instructor gone berserk? The death ship clears your port side by a hair and you see the driver for a moment. He is none of the above. Just some yuppy driving one-handed while the other cradles his car phone.

I'm not the only curmudgeon who's disenchanted with the marvel of Getting the Long Distance Feeling at 100 kilometres an hour — or in a lot of other formerly private places, for that matter. Movie patrons, restaurant customers, and public transit passengers are rising up to protest these jangly little beggars that are popping up in places that used to be peaceful and quiet. One Florida movie chain has banned the use of portable phones in all its eighteen movie houses. Bravo. Odeon and Cineplex, please copy.

I am no fan of the cellular phone phenomenon, but I have no illusions about stopping them. Car phones are so popular they've spawned their own sub-industry. Commuter Products Corporation, of Emeryville, California, offers a whole line of car phone accessories, including in-car electronic message boards, clipboards that attach to the steering wheel, and even, so help me, fax machines that fit right under the dashboard.

What next? Well, Phonevision, of course. The day is coming — or so we are threatened — when you'll have to dress up to answer the phone, because whoever's calling will be able to see you as well as talk to you.

Include me out. As a matter of fact, there's only one telephone accessory I still lust after.

You folks can buy up all the cordless phones if you want. I've got my name in for a phoneless cord.

What Ever Happened to Dear Old Ernestine?

"If the Phone Doesn't Ring, It's Me"
— Jimmy Buffet song title

IT PROBABLY SOUNDS A TAD GHOULISH, but every once in a while I entertain the fantasy of resurrecting Alexander Graham Bell, grabbing him by the nape of his mouldy winding sheet, shaking him briskly, and shouting, "There! See what you started? Are you satisfied?"

It's the telephones, Mr. Bell's most enduring legacy. They're everywhere. Americans make more than 350 million telephone calls every day. I'm pretty sure that citizen for citizen, Canadians are even gabbier, but I can't prove it. I called the Public Relations Department of Bell Canada to find out the Canadian figures.

The receptionist put me on hold.

But who needs statistics? A decent pair of eyes will tell you that we live in a plague of telephones and the little beggars continue to multiply like minks in heat.

When I was growing up, the telephone was a huge wooden affair about the size of a gum machine, featuring brass bells, a gooseneck speaker, and a crank on the side that summoned the operator. Telephones were *furniture* back then. And there was one to a household.

If you were lucky.

Nowadays, it's more like one to a room. We've got telephones in the living room and telephones in the den. There are kitchen telephones and bedroom telephones and patio telephones. The last hotel room I rented featured a telephone set into the tile wall right next to the john.

I can't begin to tell you how little I would appreciate, while in the john, a telephone call inviting me to subscribe to *Maclean's* magazine.

And you can't get away from phones by fleeing out the front door. They've invaded our cars. Last summer, I couldn't figure out why, even though traffic jams were more frequent, the traffic-bound drivers around me seemed less hostile. There was much less horn-honking, cursing, and waving of fists. Then I twigged. The drivers were less hostile because they were busy yakking into their cellular car phones. Calling up their stockbrokers or their mistresses.

Or the local radio station to deliver an on-the-spot report of a traffic jam.

Last year, Air Canada announced that soon their passengers would be able to take and receive telephone calls while they were flying, right in their seats. To which I can only offer a lukewarm "whoopee." The only two things I liked about air travel was the complimentary wine with dinner and the certain knowledge that, for the duration of the flight, I would be beyond the reach of that jarring dingaling of a jangling telephone.

No more, alas. We are succumbing to terminal telephonitis. The planet is gradually being cocooned in a sarcophagus of telephone wire. The music of the spheres will be replaced by a dial tone. A new religion will sweep the globe. Christianity, Islam, Judaism, Buddhism — all the orthodox faiths will tumble into the crypt of history, while humanity in its billions will rush to embrace the new doctrine.

The Gospel According to Ernestine.

You think I'm overreacting? That's because you haven't heard the latest news. The federal communications department is licensing field trials of the Zone Phone. It's a lightweight, cordless gizmo about the size of your TV channel zapper. It folds small enough to slip in your shirt pocket and it's called "the poor man's cellular phone." Why? Because it costs about one-twentieth the price, that's why. Experts predict it'll sell for about $150.

You realize what this means? It means that virtually everybody will be able to afford their own portable phone. Which in turn means that the only time we'll be free from ringing telephones is when we're nude in the sauna.

Well, that's not quite true. The Zone Phone is cheap because it doesn't do some of the things a regular phone does. For instance, you can make a call on the Zone Phone, but you can't receive one.

A phone that doesn't receive calls. What a concept!

I wonder if they take trade-ins.

Phones on Wheels

I DON'T KNOW YOUR POSITION on car phones, but I am pretty confident that my rust bucket will never sport one. As far as I'm concerned, one of the few remaining joys of the road is knowing that I can run to my car from time to time and make myself unphoneable for as long as there's gas in the tank.

Besides, there's something supremely arrogant about the car phone user — or at least the ones I see tooling down the highway, with their heads crooked at a 45-degree angle cradling the phone between their ear and their shoulder. Here's a guy (and it always is a guy, isn't it?) who's willing to risk your life and mine by driving one-handed while he checks in with his bookie or his insurance agent or his secretary, or for all we know, all three.

On the other hand, it is part of my burden in life to have to try to drive in and out of Toronto several times a month. During what is inexplicably called the Rush Hour . . . a period of transportational purgatory that always lasts much longer than a mere sixty minutes. And never, ever rushes.

If I had to drive in that rush hour every day, I think I just might want a phone in my car. Not just for the business calls you could take care of while you wait for the police to remove that tractor-trailer from the roadway, but to make those survival calls as well. To let Revenue Canada know you have your income tax ready but that it may be some days before you can get to a mailbox. To enjoy a little quality conference call with the kids. And to persuade your spouse not to have you declared a Missing Person.

But naw . . . in balance I'm agin 'em. Driving is scary enough these days without bringing the Bell operator into the cockpit. I think car phones should be illegal — at least until they come up with one that allows the driver to keep both hands on the wheel while he's yakking.

The British are not amused by car phones. A recent British budget levied a whopping great tax on what the chancellor of the exchequer sneeringly referred to as "yuppy phones." Chancellor Norman Lamont went further. He called them "one of the greatest scourges of modern life." And he wasn't merely talking about safety on the roads. Chancellor Lamont was declaring war on all those thoughtless twits who haul out their cellular phones in buses, planes, restaurants, and even theatres to engage in noisy chit-chat with nameless strangers concerning business about which we involuntary eavesdroppers know nothing about and couldn't care less.

It would be satisfying, a whopping tax, but not as good as an outright ban. I'd ride higher in the driver's seat if I knew for sure that the BMW bearing down on me wasn't piloted by a guy having an argument with his lawyer or his wife. Let's get rid of 'em, I say.

And what would all those suddenly phoneless yuppies do with their pent-up urge to chatter? Same as we perennially phoneless wretches have always done. Sing along with the radio.

You ever hear my Conway Twitty impression?

106

Music to My Years

H IP-WISE, LET ME PRESENT my credentials right off the top. Well, that's the first thing. I have nothing on top. I'm bald. I am also half a century old, white, mortgaged, driver of a station wagon, and charge card beholden.

Which is to say . . . square, sorta.

I can perform a one-knuckle version of "Dragnet" on the piano and slap down a pretty mean bongo on the dashboard whenever my car radio plays the theme from "Peter Gunn."

Vocally, I am . . . well, mellower than Roseanne.

So much for my hit parade with-it-ness. But once there was a time. Once I surfed on the breaking wave of popcult Cool. The memory is as clear as a Norman Rockwell painting. I was lying on the rec-room floor in my parents' suburban home. Plaster ducks on the walls. *Reader's Digest*s and *Maclean's* on the Lemon Pledged coffee table.

The Dorsey Brothers were on the black-and-white TV in the corner. Tommy — or maybe it was Jimmy — was introducing a new entertainer. I left off counting the threads in the rug and glanced at the box.

Suddenly my pubescent body twitched in sympathetic spasms. Tears of joy gallumphed down my cheeks.

My father's reaction was more phlegmatic. "What the hell is *that?*" he grumbled.

That was the first national TV appearance of a twenty-one-year-old Memphis truck driver. The Elvis phenomenon would shortly tattoo a spidery hairline fracture right across the North American psyche, with us kids on one side of the crack, all adults on the other. My father — heck, every parent I knew — could never understand what Elvis was All About. "The man doesn't sing — he yells!" "Can't even understand the words!" "I could play a guitar better'n that!"

That was an eon ago. Now, I have kids who lie on the living-room rug and watch TV — music videos mostly. Which were unheard-of in my day. Can you imagine Elvis making a music video of, say, "Blue Suede Shoes"?

Not that the video would have to have anything to do with shoes or suede or blue. The fairy tales that music videos spin never have anything to do with the music. As a matter of fact, I think the purpose of music videos is to hide the music — which is just as well, because frankly most of the music video stars can't sing. I mean, even if you put your ear right against the TV, you can't make out the words. As for their musical ability, listen: I can play bongos on my car dash—

Omigawd.

I sound just like my father.

Camcorderphobia

G OT YOUR CAMCORDER YET? If not, I figure there's just you and me left, chum. Camcorders are the fastest-selling item down at my local camera shop, and that's pretty well the story right across the country. Customers are snapping them up faster than whisky-jacks at a bush barbecue. I went to a wedding last weekend where every third guest was coming on like Francis Ford Coppolla, prowling around the reception with camcorders screwed to their eyesockets, each trying to find a special angle or a unique shot. The world's gone video camera crazy.

I don't figure I'll ever buy one. I'd have to sponsor a Taiwanese factory hand to come over and brief me every time I wanted to use the thing. Here's a brochure description of a new camcorder I could call mine for a mere $1,699.99:

"AM/FM Hi-Fi with built-in Stereo Mic. 8:1 power zoom lens with Macro. 4 Mode Program AE (Auto Exposure). Variable High Speed Shutter (27 speeds, up to 1/10,000 sec.) Clean/Still/Slow/Frame Advance. 2-Page Digital Superimposer."

I don't know if they're selling me a video camera or a Chalk River atom smasher.

This is bewildering stuff for a guy who was raised on the Kodak Brownie box camera. The Kodak Brownie, I recall, had precisely three features: a knob that you cranked to advance the film; a hole that you pointed at whatever you were taking a picture of; and a hole that you peered into to make sure your subject was centred, smiling, and not picking its nose.

And that was it! A camera so simple a chimpanzee could operate it. Compare that to the above-mentioned camcorder, which has lenses and eyepieces and microphones and display panels and more buttons, dials, knobs, turrets, bells, and whistles than the dashboard of the Millennium Falcon.

Doesn't seem to faze the younger generation, though. They've taken to camcorders as easily and enthusiastically as my generation took to Elvis. In parts of the U.S., kids are allowed to hand in "video" term papers now. They go through encyclopaedia film footage stored on optical disc, dub off what they want, edit the result, throw on a voice-over narration, and hey, presto! A term paper, hi-tech nineties style.

Recently, some Calgary schoolkids got to commute in comfort aboard "video buses" equipped with video monitors and VCRs.

Which means that students with their own camcorders could watch replays of recess all the way home from school.

That's another reason I don't plan to buy a camcorder. I think it's a fad. It's going to go the way of the sack dress and the Hula Hoop. Because ultimately all the camcorder offers is replays. And how many of those can you watch?

Sure, the baby's first steps, the graduation ceremony, Niagara Falls, weddings, picnics . . . but then what?

Life is not about reruns. It's about going on, not living in the past.

Carlton Fisk knows that. Back in the mid-seventies Fisk belted a homer in a World Series game that became a classic, like Bobby Orr's floating-through-the-air Stanley Cup winning goal. Since then, Fisk's famous home run has been a replay feature of just about every baseball retrospective aired on TV. I've seen it dozens of times. Bet you have too.

But Carlton Fisk hasn't. He refuses to watch it. "I turn it off or go out of the room whenever it comes along," he says. "I want to keep it fresh in my head. I want to keep hold of the memory of what it felt like, as opposed to what it looks like on the screen."

Ah. What it felt like. A wise man, that Mr. Fisk. Wouldn't be surprised to learn that he doesn't even own a camcorder.

Rocket Radio

I'VE GOT A LOT OF GIZMOS in my life. A pocket knife with a pair of scissors in it. A bicycle with more speeds than I can use. A fishing reel that theoretically lets line out and reels it back in with maximum efficiency, and a telephone answering machine that tells me who phoned while I was out in the back yard trying to unsnag my fishing reel. I've got a remote TV channel changer, windshield wipers that work, a pair of running shoes with silicone implants to ease my corns . . . I've got a lotta gizmos in my life, but the one I'm fondest of is the one I'm fondling right now.

It's made of red and white plastic, it's about five inches long, shaped like a Buck Rogers rocketship, and it's at least thirty-five years old. It's a radio. Well, it's sort of a radio. First one I had. It has two wires hanging off it. One is an earphone and the other is a rudimentary antenna that ends in an alligator clip.

I pop the earphone in my ear, clip the alligator clip to a, well, say one of those big old hot-water radiators you used to find in houses three or four decades ago, I clip it to that, twiddle the nose cone in and out, and you know what I can hear? I can hear Russ Germaine. I can hear Allana Campbell. I can hear Lister Sinclair and Clyde Gilmour and Murray McLauchlan.

Or I could. Truth is, I haven't sat down and fooled around with this gizmo in — oh, must be thirty years now.

But I used to listen to it every night. I could pick up Guy Lombardo and the Voice of Doom, Lorne Green. Great old shows like "Boston Blackie," "Amos 'n' Andy," "Suspense" . . .

Thing is, there's no dial on this rocket radio. You just jiggled the nose cone till something intelligible came swimming through the static. But that kind of added to the excitement. You never knew what you'd get to hear.

Sure, it was scattergun listening and the sound was tinny at best. But look at the plus side — no tuner, no turntable, no tweeters or woofers — no batteries, even. I spent a lot of hours hunched over by the hot-water rad manipulating my rocket radio. And I missed a lot of radio refinements. I never owned a hi-fi. I missed shower radios and boom boxes, Walkmans and of course CD players. Which isn't a bad thing, as it turns out. I hear that CD players, less than ten years old, are already slated for the scrap heap. Couple of years ago it was announced that a new system, DAT — digital audio tape — would render the compact disc as relevant as the Hula Hoop.

Ah, but that was a couple of years ago. Now DAT's dead as a dodo, eclipsed by something called the DCC — the digital compact cassette. Wanna make any guesses as to the shelf life of the DCC?

As far as I'm concerned, the CDs and DCCs and DATs can all RIP. I'm not going to play this game and neither is my credit card.

I think I'll just stick with my rocket radio, if you don't mind.

Now, if I could just find one of those great old-fashioned hot-water radiators . . .

Chuckles in a Can

AWAY BACK IN 1925 a photographer by the name of Marcus Adams made a prediction. He said, "Someday soon, Mr. Photography is going to marry Miss Wireless, and heaven help everybody when they get married. Life will be very complicated."

Mr. Adams was right. It would be another quarter of a century before photographic images and wireless radio publicly tied the knot, but they did. And became television. And changed the way we looked at each other forever.

Or don't look at each other. Last summer I stayed at a bed and breakfast in the country. One evening when it was too rainy to go for a walk I decided to join the family in their parlour. They'd said guests were welcome to drop in anytime. The whole family was in the parlour watching TV. Avidly. It was like stumbling across a band of Neanderthals paying homage to some flickering idol. Nobody smiled at newcomers or greeted them, they just silently made room on the couch. People came and went with no hi or goodbye. What, and interrupt the sacred TV service?

The worst thing was the *aloneness* of it all. That parlour could have had twelve people in it, and they still wouldn't have been *with* each other. We'd all have been . . . alone together, each mesmerized by the cathode campfire in the corner.

A strange phenomenon, the boob tube. Marcus Adams was a prescient man foreseeing television twenty-five years before its time. But could even Marcus be expected to believe Arsenio Hall? The Shoppers' Channel? "The Love Connection"?

I'd really like to hear what he thought of the concept of laugh tracks.

Canned laughter. Here's a grisly thought for you: when you hear those guffaws and chortles and belly laughs in the background of an episode of "Growing Pains" or "Three's Company," who are you really hearing?

Answer: dead people. Those are the laughs of ghosts. They're recordings of long-gone audiences taped at old George Burns and Gracie Allen or "Fibber McGee and Molly" shows.

Or maybe even an ancient Abbott and Costello movie. That famous comedic duo once took out an insurance policy with Lloyd's of London to cover themselves in case anybody in their audience should die of laughter. We don't worry about whether they laugh. We've got canned laughter for that.

I guess canned laughter makes TV producers sleep easier, but it doesn't say much for our collective sense of humour — and it doesn't say much for the value we put on our free time either.

The psychiatrist R. D. Laing once wrote: "I am told the average Canadian watches television for five hours a day. Would they be any worse off for staring at a blank wall?"

Well of course we would, R. D.

Blank walls don't tell you when they're being funny.

Return to Sender

R OGER LOGAN IS A BUSINESS executive who popped up in my
local newspaper not too long ago. He was judged newswor-
thy because he opined publicly that most Canadians don't mind
receiving junk mail at all. On the contrary, says Mr. Logan, "it's a
status symbol to be on all those lists."

C'mon, Roger. I haven't taken an exhaustive survey, but I have
never personally met anybody who enjoys getting junk mail.

I suppose MacMillan Bloedel and Great Lakes Paper executives
nod approvingly in the direction of junk mail. I imagine lumber-
jacks and offset printers and typographers and graphic artists think
it's swell, but I have yet to encounter anybody winnowing their
mail down at the post office, crowing, "Oh great! A chance to buy
a copper bracelet against arthritis, investment opportunities in
Florida Everglades, and a personal letter from Ed McMahon!"

I suspect that Roger Logan somewhat overstates the case for
junk mail. But then, Roger Logan is vice-president of the Herbert
A. Watts direct marketing firm — which is to say he's one of the
head demons charged with maintaining an adequate diet of junk
mail fodder for your mailbox and mine. So perhaps Roger Logan
has his own four-page, full-colour silkscreen magazine insert axe
to grind on the junk mail question. Be that as it may, the fact is,
while Roger Logan exults, you and I are drowning in a muskeg of
unwanted mail.

What, aside from cursing, crumpling, and contributing to
Canada's shrinking landfill site problem, can we do about it? We

can burn it in the fireplace, which is okay if you've got a fireplace, though no more environmentally sound, and incidentally, hard on your chimney. We can send it back where it came from, but that's time-consuming and kind of expensive.

Or we can do what Toby Sanger does. Toby is the only person other than Roger Logan I have ever heard speak positively about junk mail. In a letter to the editor, Toby said, "I now treat junk mail as a source of great opportunities and fun for the whole family." Toby introduces junk mailers by mailing one's Junk Lit to another. "I especially enjoy sending charity appeals in the return envelopes of corporate business groups," writes Toby. "The beauty is . . . this solution keeps the posties employed, puts some variety into the lives of clerical workers who open the envelopes, and allows struggling groups to reach a wider audience at the expense of the direct marketeers."

That's it. We can be social secretaries by sending half our junk mail to the senders of the other half. Don'cha love elegant solutions? Especially when they're simple, direct, and personal?

Sort of like junk mail itself.

Bring Back the Bike

O N SEPTEMBER 13, 1899, real estate agent Henry H. Bliss stepped off a streetcar at Central Park West and 74th Street, inhaled a deep double lungful of crisp New York air, and started to cross the street.

He was immediately run over and killed by a horseless carriage.

It's a very small consolation for Mr. Bliss, but his final involuntary act at least got him into the history books. He is North America's number-one traffic fatality. Officially, the first person to expire at the hands (make that bumpers) of an automobile.

He's had lots of imitators since.

Nothing kills like the car. Automobile accidents are the leading cause of death of young people. More than two million — *two million* — North Americans have died in or under cars since Henry Bliss met his fate. And more than six million have been severely injured for life.

That's not a "family convenience" — that's an unnatural disaster. Indeed, if some demented Middle East tinpot maniac ever did to us what the automobile has done to us, we'd be well into World War III by now.

If there was any justice, the U.S. Sixth Fleet would be anchored off Detroit, not Saudi Arabia.

Speaking of which, it's hard to find much good to say about the Kuwait Kerfuffle, but I did spy one cheering note. The TV showed a bunch of folks in Minneapolis demonstrating against

U.S. involvement. One of them carried a placard that read "Oil, Schmoil — Ride Your Bike."

Well, yes. If more of us took to our two-wheelers it would be worse for Saddam and better for us. Bikes don't guzzle gas, pollute the air, or suckle on government-subsidized oil prices. It's also hard to imagine a five-o'clock bicycle traffic jam or a two-Schwinn head-on, multiple-fatality bike crash.

Bikes don't kill people the way cars do.

Sure, you say, but this is Canada, dummy. You can't ride bikes in this country in the winter. Well, I've spent time in downtown Toronto for the past ten winters and every day I've seen bike couriers flashing back and forth, on fair days and foul. Last January during one of Toronto's "blizzards" (a whole three inches of snow!), the whole municipality of Mammon slithered to a halt, cars up on the sidewalks, trucks spinning their tires. Nothing moved — except the bike couriers. They were wearing motorcycle gloves and earmuffs and a Plimsoll line of dirty grey slush up past their waists, but they were moving.

And needless to say, no matter how frosty the winter morning, there's no problem getting a bike to "turn over."

As a matter of fact, bicycles are getting more and more sensible. We've been through the silly phase of ten-speeds. That's where we all bought machines with tires the width of spaghetti noodles, racing handlebars, and ultra-light, ultra-expensive space-age alloy construction — terrific for athletes like Steve Bauer, trying to shave milliseconds off his time on the Tour de France. Pretty silly for a stenographer trying to negotiate potholes and sewer grilles on her way to work. After that came mountain bikes, with eighty-six forward gears, nubbly tires that belonged on army assault vehicles, and an even more expensive space-age alloy construction so durable you could throw the bike off the top of the mountain once you'd ridden up the side of it.

Today, it's possible to buy a normal, modestly geared, modestly priced bicycle that won't win marathons or scale the Himalayas but will get your from A to B quickly and comfortably.

Me? I'm beyond that. On the cutting edge of new bike technology, actually. I ride a one-speed CCM, a balloon-tired machine of ancient vintage. It's a classic. The kind of bike our grandparents threw their legs over.

The kind Henry Bliss should have been riding on September 13, 1899.

All Choked Up

MY FRIEND FRAN TAUGHT ME a terrific new word this week. Well, it's new to me. Fran tells me the Greeks routinely kicked it around a couple of thousand years ago. It's "anagnorisis." Aristotle described it as the moment of recognition when ignorance gives way to knowledge. I like to think of anagnorisis as that moment when the metaphysical lightbulb goes on in your head. (Or in Aristotle's case, an oil lamp, maybe.) In any case, I have a fresh anagnorisis dripping all over my shirt front I'd like to share. Happened in my driveway this morning. My son was trying to start the car, which wasn't cooperating. "NNNNNnnnnnnrn," the car said. And also "nNNNNNNnnrrrrrnnn."

"Give it a little choke," I blurted. And got rewarded with the dreaded blank teenage stare. "Choke?" That's when I remembered that cars haven't featured a manual choke for the past twenty years. Anagnorisis. That moment when ignorance gives way to knowledge. I had thought, ignorantly, that I was doing okay. I recognize now that I am getting obsolete.

I'm just lucky I didn't advise him to retard the spark or ease back on the throttle or whirl the magneto. I remember all those utterly obsolete things too. Nowadays, all cars have is an ignition key. A driver's function is to slide into the driver's seat, slip the key in, and turn it to the right. And if the car doesn't go *RRRRRRRrrrrrmmmmm*, you pull the key back out, find a phone, and call CAA.

Yep, if Henry Ford were to reincarnate tomorrow at the end of an Oshawa assembly line — or for that matter in some downtown parking lot — he would have a lot of trouble reconciling what's become of what he started. Mind you, some things haven't changed. Old Henry would still find axles and wheel wells and drive shafts and rocker panels. Transmissions would be infinitely fancier but still recognizable. And we still have the dashboard, which actually predates Henry Ford. The dashboard was originally just a slab of wood or steel to protect the drivers from the gunk kicked up in their faces by "dashing" horses. Lot of holdovers from the days when real horsepower did the work. Even the name "car" is just a customized low-rider variation of "carriage" — as in horseless.

In the U.K., motorists cling even more tenaciously to automotive traditions. Brits murmur of windscreens and bonnets and boots. I'll bet a British kid wouldn't scowl if the old man advised him to give it a little choke.

I should have taken Erma Bombeck's advice. Erma's an American comedian, mother, and motorist, not necessarily in that order. The Bombeck driving dictum: Never lend your car to anyone to whom you have given birth.

Black's addendum:

Especially if they don't know what a choke is.

The Jetcar — Who Needs It?

> *In our worship of the machine, we have settled for*
> *something less than a full life, something that is*
> *hardly even a tenth of life, or a hundredth of a life.*
> *We have confused progress with mechanization.*
>
> — Lewis Mumford

DO YOU REMEMBER THE MACHINES they promised us? You'd have to be a certain age to recall them — say, forty or over. I used to read all about them in *Popular Mechanics*. That magazine had a near-fetish about the "automobiles of the future." Time and again the editors would devote full cover stories to rhapsodic predictions of just how wonderful transportation was soon going to be. Graphic artists were commissioned to sketch Star Trekkish metropoli bristling with futuristic hives and domes, all interlaced with translucent walkways and moving sidewalks. Whizzing through the air in all directions you could see the "automobiles" of the future — compact saucers, really, about the size of a midsize American car, but capable of travelling overland or through the air. Each of the cars had a plastic bubble of a cockpit, and in that cockpit you could usually see a grinning, middle-class nuclear family of the future, out for a care-free weekend spin.

I used to moon over those articles in *Popular Mechanics* back in the late fifties. They always assured us this fantastic world was just around the corner. We'd all be flitting about in jetcars well before the turn of the century — by 1980 at the very latest.

Well, it's getting on for the millennium, and I often think of those long-overdue Jetcars as my hopelessly old-fashioned, terminally pavement-bound Toyota noses into the morning rush-hour traffic going to the city. I've usually got plenty of time to think, because I'm fused into a miles-long traffic jam that's going nowhere.

Still, it's a chance to work out some great finger-drum solos on the steering wheel while I listen to the radio. During the really bad traffic jams I even get to read a bit of the morning paper.

Which is where I came across the story about Paul Moller and his M200X. That's the rather un-catchy name Paul's bestowed on his invention. There's a photograph of him in the M200X that accompanies the newspaper story.

I would have named his invention differently.

I would have called it the Jetcar.

Because that's what it is, all right. Ten years late and not quite as swanky as the *Popular Mechanics* artist's conception, but it's a jetcar, and Paul Moller, a professor of aeronautics, is in the cockpit, hovering about ten feet off the ground while newspaper reporters take pictures.

The M200X is only the beginning, says Moller. His California company is already working on a model that will carry four passengers at 500 miles an hour as high as 30,000 feet and as far as 800 miles on a single tank of gas.

Just as *Popular Mechanics* predicted back in the fifties!

So how come I'm not excited?

Perhaps it's the price tag. Moller says a copy of his M200X will cost about the same as a helicopter — and that's a lot for a craft that so far has managed to hover only about 30 feet off the ground for less than three minutes.

Or maybe it's the realization that Jetcars will only make driving worse, not better.

It's bad enough being stuck to the pavement, worrying about tanker trucks coming up your tailpipe and muscle cars passing you on a hill. Can you imagine being out for a romantic drive with your Sweet Patootie when suddenly the blood drains from her face, her eyes bulge like Westinghouse 60-Watters, and she shrieks, "Yuppy on his carphone at twelve o'clock high!"

You go ahead, Mr. Moller. I'll sit this one out.

Automatic Auto Parking

I F I HAD TO PICK MY FAVOURITE autocrat, I think I'd give the nod to Henry Ford. He gets my vote for a single sentence he uttered way back in the early years of the century when his Model A's were knocking the socks off the horse and buggy era. Somebody asked Mr. Ford what colours his new auto-mobiles came in. Mr. Ford said, "Son, you can have any colour you like, as long as it's black."

Simplicity. I like that in a tycoon.

I like simplicity in a car too. I wish I'd been around when Mr. Ford's first creations were king of the highway. They sound like my kind of car. My dad had one. He said when he couldn't buy gas for his Model T, he used to throw a jug of kerosene in the gas tank. Said it ran just about as well. He also kept a hammer under the front seat for minor off-road car repairs. If something went wrong and the car quit on him, he just pulled over to the shoulder, lifted the hood, and took a swing with the hammer. Usually worked, he said.

You remember when cars were simple? When a dashboard didn't feature anything much more complicated than a speedometer, a heater switch, a choke, and on the real fancy models, a cigarette lighter? Nowadays, dashboards feature tachometers and air-conditioners and cruise controls and cassette decks, AM/FM radios, rear window defrosters, windshield spritzers, CD players, and on the real fancy models . . . no cigarette lighter.

Well, it's going to get worse, friends. Even as I speak, a group of lab-coated technicians armed with clipboards are standing around a gull-winged prototype automobile of the future — called the Integrated Research Futura Concept Car — in a top-secret testing facility on the outskirts of New York. As they stand there, murmuring into their microcassette recorders, the sleek IRFC car pulls to a stop in front of an open curb space between two other automobiles. The driver gets out, closes the door, and walks away. Then the car parks. Itself.

Kid you not. It's called the Automatic Parking System. A battery of tiny electric eyes located above the bumpers and along the flanks of the car feed proximity data — which is to say, how close the car is to scraping the curb or bunting the for and aft vehicles — into an onboard computer. The computer activates the steering column and the accelerator, transmission, and brakes as required. The car parks itself.

Now, there's a good deal of heavy irony idling at the curb here. The company that owns the Integrated Research Futura Concept Car is Volkswagen. The very people who gave us, once upon a time, the Volkswagen Bug, the car I think came closest to Henry Ford's original ideal of simplicity and reliability. The Bug was doomed. It was cheap to operate, reliable, and it didn't wear out nearly fast enough. The automakers buried the Bug as soon as they decently could and went on to blue-sky concepts like the Integrated Research Futura Concept Car. The one with the Automatic Parking System. Which, when it becomes available, is expected to add anywhere from $6,000 to $12,000 to the car sticker price. Which is about six to twelve times more than Henry Ford charged for an entire tin lizzie.

And I'll betcha when they do come out, you'll be able to buy the Integrated Research Futura Concept Car in any colour you want. As long as it isn't black.

Carsnatching

B EST CAR I EVER HAD in my life was an ancient footlocker-green, two-door, stickshift Volvo with a wonky windshield wiper and a front bumper held on with a twist of barbed wire.

Fast? That jalopy couldn't catch a wheelchair in a quarter mile.

Stylish? I've seen sexier manure spreaders.

Mint condition? My Volvo had more dings and dents than a Boston Bruin defenceman.

That crate was clunky, arthritic, homely, and slow as a sea slug in peanut butter — and I loved it like family. Why?

Because that was the whole point! My car was so utterly and demonstrably worthless that I never had to worry about it being swiped! Every year I bought the least amount of insurance I could get away with, and every time I climbed out of that car I left doors unlocked, windows down — keys in the ignition, even.

When I came back, it would always be where I left it. And I knew it would be.

Even car thieves have certain standards, you know.

Nowadays, I drive an almost new car, and like all the good car-owning burghers around me, I'm neurotic about scratches and dents and whether or not I locked both back doors.

It's stupid, fretting over an overpriced agglomeration of chrome and plastic on wheels. I'd like to be more Zen-like, less material-istic, but there it is. If God has a sense of humour, he'll have me snuffed in a head-on collision on my way home from having my car Turtle Waxed.

126

Well, if I am an auto-neurotic, at least I'm part of a trend. There's a whole new industry out there, dedicated to people just like me.

Consider Gregory. He comes from a firm called Sharper Image. Gregory is tall, well built, and handsome in a rugged, don't-mess-with-me kind of way. You want to do some shopping but you're afraid to leave your car in a high-crime area? Take Gregory along. He'd be glad to sit in your car all day — and all night too, if you want.

Well, he won't actually be "glad" to do it. Truth to tell, Gregory doesn't give much of a damn one way or the other. That's because Gregory is a mannequin. A dummy. But an extremely realistic one. "His strong masculine image," says a Sharper Image spokesman, "makes Gregory the ideal companion for single women, night nurses, the elderly, or the handicapped."

Sure — but can he fix flats and will he spring for half the gas?

Over in England, authorities are turning downright devious in their war against car thieves. In cities such as Liverpool, Manchester, Birmingham, and Leeds, lightfingered Louies on the lookout for some free transportation are frequently coming across some very sporty autos, completely unlocked, with the keys in the ignition.

Scarcely believing their luck, they jump into the car, turn the key, and — BWEEP BWEEP BWEEP!

Suddenly, all Hades breaks loose. The engine cuts off, the windows whoosh up, and the door locks snap shut. And all the while a 120-decibel klaxon is ringing the thief's head senseless. Meanwhile, the local constabulary has been electronically alerted and cops are on their way to arrest the carnapper and escort him to an institution where he will have no need of anybody's car keys for some time.

The U.S.–Russian cold war may be over, but the cops 'n' robbers crusade wages on undimmed. When the good guys come up with something new, it works only as long as it takes the crooks to figure out how to short-circuit it.

I can see it all now. Some night soon an alarm bell will flash CAR THEFT IN PROGRESS on a British police switchboard. The bobbies fly out of the station, surround the car, yank open the driver's door, grab the thief, sling him to the sidewalk — and find themselves staring down at the strong, masculine, don't-mess-with-me smirk of . . .

Gregory, British version, patent pending.

Planet Earth: Patent Pending

I HAVE A COMPUTERIZED DIGITAL clock on the dashboard of my car. It reads 3P. Or sometimes :19. That's all it's said since way back in April when we were supposed to set the clocks ahead from Daylight Savings. That's the day I tried to adjust my dashboard clock by toggling the little black nodules on its side. I screwed it up, and now whenever I look at my clock all it tells me is 3P. Or occasionally :19.

The thing that kills me is that one of these days one of my teenagers will get in the car, and I'll grumble about the stupid damn clock, and he or she will reach over, palpate the buttons almost absent-mindedly for a couple of seconds, and my clock will be working again.

Kids *get* computer stuff. Even devices they've never read the instruction manuals for. Adults (at least the pre-silicone-chip boobs and klutzes I hang around with) don't.

Near as I can figure, computer-sensitivity represents an absolute sea-change in the evolution of humanity, right up there on a level with the invention of the wheel. For hundreds of thousands of years, *Homo sapiens* shuffled around, dragging his baggage behind him. Then some Neolithic hotshot discovered that if you lopped off two sections of a log and stuck an axle through them, you could make a cart, hitch it to a donkey, climb aboard, and sightsee while the donkey did the work.

And I'll betcha a dollar to a solid stone doughnut that when that guy invented the wheel, there were a dozen older lowbrows sitting stubbornly in the mouths of their caves, picking their teeth with mastodon bones, and grumbling that the newfangled wheel thing was crazy and just didn't make sense.

I think computer consciousness is in the same league. I sit in my car, confounded by a simple computerized clock, while my kids look at a laptop with about as much wonder as I feel for a couch pillow.

Kids accept that a wafer of plastic half the size of a roof shingle can contain twenty-four volumes of the *Encyclopaedia Britannica*, fifty years of unemployment statistics for western Manitoba, plus a graph chart of the number of times the word "aardvark" appears in Beatles songs. They know that computers can plop them into a steamy safari down the Zambezi or the cockpit of a 747 landing at O'Hare International.

It's even bigger than that. Maxis Corporation now offers a computer game called SimEarth. SimEarth allows you to create a planet. Start life. Play God. With SimEarth software and a keyboard, you take a lifeless planet and brew up a biological soup to taste. You create dinosaurs and cockroaches; oceans and continents. Oops! Don't like the way those two-legged pink critters are messing things up? No problem — edit. Choose from War, Pestilence, Earthquakes, or Massive Meteor Strikes. Just press *A* for the Apocalypse menu.

Exciting stuff for a computer-compatible kid. Scary stuff for an adult Luddite who can't manage his own dashboard clock. I have visions of some other faraway ethereal father figure handing his son a disk marked SimEarth and saying, "It's still an hour to go before supper, God — why don't you go play on the computer?"

The Destructor

THE LESSON TODAY CONCERNS euphemisms. Linguistic Muzak. The pretty words and punchless phrases we use to cushion and deodorize our thoughts.

"Passing on" is a popular euphemism. So much softer and unfinal than "dying," "croaking," or "biting the dust."

"Expecting" — there's another dandy euphemism. It's vague and sexless, unlike such straightforward vulgarisms as "pregnant," "in calf," or "carrying a bun in the oven."

The military world is a veritable compost heap of euphemisms. They're the folks who gave us the "anti-personnel device" (read lethal explosive designed to shred flesh and pulverize bone). And who can forget "nuclear deterrent" (read annihilation of life coupled with long-term planet poisoning)?

There's another euphemism currently making the rounds. It's a real late-twentieth-century cutie.

"Sanitary landfill."

Roll it around on your tongue once or twice. Sanitary landfill. Might almost be the name of a new complexion cream. "Sanitary" — nice, clean, inoffensive adjective. "Landfill" — something to enrich the soil and eradicate all those unseemly pocks and craters.

It sounds almost as if we're doing the world a favour.

In fact, we're unloading our crap.

Shrink wrap, old supermarket bags, bald tires, rusty bedsprings, breakfast crusts, cat litter — not to mention greases, solvents, acids, alkalies, and a mad chemist's brew of toxic, cancerous gunk too various to catalogue.

And if we can believe the headlines, we're running out of places to bury the stuff. The city of Toronto, that megalomaniacatropolis on the barely flowing Humber, is currently dispatching outriders to most of the townships and counties within garbage-hauling distance of its borders. They hope to strike a deal with somebody — *any*body — who will agree to take Hogtown's garbage.

Toronto's not alone. There's not a Canadian city or town of any consequence that has to look too deeply into its municipal crystal ball to see the garbage piling up.

And this is in Canada, an underpopulated country with nearly four million square miles of back yard!

Makes you wonder what they do in less capacious countries. Is Portugal sinking under the weight of its trash? Is Belgium up to its eavestroughs in Glad Bags? What about England?

Actually, we don't have to wonder about one city in England. An ex-citizen of Nottingham recently wrote an explanatory letter to the editor of a Toronto newspaper.

The letter writer, one Ben Banham, recalled walking to school past a building known as the Destructor. Inside the building, "the waste was dumped on conveyor belts and sorted by hand. All metal was first removed, except cans, and sent to scrap metal yards. Butcher bones were sorted out and finished as bonemeal for gardens; bottles and glass jars were removed and recycled. The remainder went through the furnace and finished as ashes and cans. The cans were boiled and went to steel mills. That left tons of ashes, which had two uses. They were mixed with cement and made into cinder blocks . . . [which] were used to line the inside of the brick-built houses, also as partition walls inside, and plastered . . .

"It would be fair to say," writes Mr. Banham, "that scores of the numerous soccer stadiums in the country used tons of the ashes for several inches of drainage under the turf. Result: Nothing wasted."

Indeed. Mr. Banham says the Destructor handled and disposed of all the garbage of Nottingham, an industrialized city of 300,000.

But Mr. Banham is wrong on one count. Something was wasted: the lesson we ought to have learned from Nottingham.

Ben Banham is a senior citizen and the Destructor is a hazy memory. All the facts and figures cited above were true only when Ben Banham was a Nottingham lad.

And that was eighty years ago.

PART 4

Destination: TBA

All Lined Up with No Place to Go

THERE ARE A FEW LARGELY inescapable unpleasant facts of life in this the dog-end of the twentieth century. There is the common cold, there is the Victor Kiam commercial, and there are lineups.

You would think a civilization that can toss up sixty-storey office buildings and take candid snapshots of Jupiter's backside could solve a simple commonplace irritation like the everyday lineup. But no. For all our sophistication and progress and technical knowhow, we still line up. We line up for movies. We line up for bank tellers. We line up in cafeterias and bus stations and airports and at supermarket checkouts.

I've been lining up for tickets or buses or at gas pumps all my life. We all have. Lining up is such a natural feature of human life that whole cultures have special ways of doing it. Canadians line up. New Yorkers stand on line. Britons politely queue. Germans pretend to line up until a door actually opens or a clerk appears. Then they turn into rabid berserkers, elbowing and kicking with a passion seldom seen outside a Stanley Cup playoff.

Nowhere are lineups more cleverly disguised than at Disney World in Florida.

For one thing, Disney World lineups don't look like lineups. They zig-zag back and forth. Somebody flying over Disney World and looking down might get the impression he was looking at a bunch of snakes digesting venetian blinds.

So you stand. Stand and shuffle. Shuffle in a zig-zag that allows you to pass the same family from Dubuque sixteen times while you wait to get into the Epcot Center. It also disguises the fact that you will actually walk three and a half miles before you get to pay for your ticket.

At the checkout counters in Sloans supermarkets in New York, two magicians work the lineups amusing customers by pulling rabbits out of hats and handkerchiefs out of thin supermarket air.

Well, I dunno. Beats staring at the fluorescent lights or counting the cans in the pork and bean display, I suppose. But personally, I'd prefer it if they'd put the money they pay the magicians into hiring a couple of extra cashiers instead. I could keep the magicians busy balancing my chequebook. There's an operation that really calls for sleight of hand.

Is there anything good about lineups? Well, they give us comedy material from time to time. You heard the joke about the Russian standing in an interminable lineup in front of the Moscow vodka store? He's been there for hours and hours. Finally he can't stand it any longer, throws down his hat, and shouts, "I'm fed up! I'm going home to get my rifle and shoot the vodka commissar!"

Two hours later the man returns, meekly takes his place at the back of the line. "What happened?" the others ask.

"Oh well," he says, "this lineup is shorter than the lineup to shoot the commissar."

The simple fact is, we human beings might have been better off if we'd spent more time lining up and less time lying down doing what we do best — multiplying. There are too many of us. The party's getting crowded. And that means more lineups. Experts have calculated that by the middle of the next century, humans will be spending up to 20 percent of their waking hours lined up waiting for something or other.

Well, I probably won't be around in 2050 to see how long the lineups are, but I'll do what I can for you youngsters. I'll put in a word with St. Peter when I meet him at the gate.

Mind you, I'm taking a good book with me.

Just in case there's a lineup.

The Subway: It Can Take Your Breath Away

When you ride the subway twice a day, it's difficult to think of the immortal soul.

— Anonymous

THIS IS THE WAY it shapes up worldwide. There are only forty in existence and/or on the drawing boards. America has seven, the former Soviet Union has six, Canada has two. New York boasts the biggest one. Moscow has the cleanest, Montreal the quietest. Toronto's is forty years old — but that's a mere pup compared to the one in London, England, which dates back to 1863.

People who use them every day curse and roll their eyes at the very mention of them, but when I was a little kid fresh from the country, the thought of a ride on the subway was the thrill of a lifetime.

Subways. It would be tough to explain the concept to an ancient Roman, say.

"Well, Cicero, what we're gonna do is dig this long tunnel right under the city, see, and lay in some tracks so we can stuff people into long steel tubes and move 'em around the city quickly. It's sorta like an underground aquaduct for working stiffs."

Subways are hideously expensive to build, horrible to live next to, and, once the thrill wears off, not that enchanting to use. But they are wonderfully efficient at doing what they were designed to do — ferry huge rafts of people quickly and easily from one part of a metropolis to another. In fact, it's hard to imagine how cities like New York, London, Paris, or Toronto would even

139

function if you took out the subways. Surface traffic in those cities already grinds to a halt several times each working day. If the tens of thousands of underground molepeople suddenly surfaced, got in their cars and trucks or started hailing taxis, the cities would go into permanent gridlock. One has only to stand by the door at Toronto's Yonge and Bloor station about eight-thirty of a weekday morning watching the waves of commuters changing subway trains to appreciate what above-ground horrors the subway saves us from.

Mind you, there is a price. On a personal discomfort scale, riding the subway on a hot day during rush hour is only about two notches above root canal work. The wheels screech like tortured souls. The drivers time their lurches diabolically to catch you off balance and send you tumbling into the stolid Black Panther sitting across from you. If you are shoehorned sardine-like into a standing room only car, you discover that the man wedged behind you is (a) oversexed and (b) had onions for breakfast.

Which brings up one other hurdle that must be surmounted by every veteran strap-hanger:

The olfactory factor.

Subways, to put it gently, stink. Or rather, a significant percentage of the folks who ride them do. A regular subway commuter encounters more B.O. than the towel boy at a World Wrestling Federation tag team match.

The city of Madrid has an appallingly pungent subway system called El Metro. Garlic is a particularly popular commodity in Madrid — much more popular than, say, underarm deodorant. Officials handle the resulting problem in an unusually forthright way. About three times a day, a guy strolls through the subway trains with a spray nozzle in his hand and a cylinder of cheap cologne on his back. Everybody gets hosed down. And you know what? You're grateful.

In London's Underground, they've taken to popping little sachets of sweet-smelling fragrances under the seats to mask the malodorousness of the clientele.

I don't know if officials in Toronto or Montreal plan to fumigate their rolling stock, but they have my vote.

In the meantime, let's you and me do our bit. Let's make a pledge to bathe or shower faithfully before we ride any city's underground rails. Do I have your word? Thank you. That's an approving smile on my face.

You just can't see it because of the gas mask.

What Ever Happened to the Passion Pit?

T HE FIRST ONE IN THE WORLD opened in Camden, New Jersey, back in 1932.

The last one — in my neck of the woods, anyway — closed on October 20, 1991.

Drive-in movies, I'm talking about. Or Park-In Theatre, as that first New Jersey one was awkwardly called. It wasn't much. Just a big sheet of canvas hoisted over the roof of a scuzzy machine shop on the outskirts of Camden. The hopeful proprietor had bulldozed flat a field in front of the screen, creating parking space for four hundred cars.

On opening night, fourteen showed up. Each driver paid 25 cents for the privilege of squinting at a forgettable feature-length piece of fluff entitled *Wife Beware*.

It was a lousy flick, but then, whoever went to the drive-in for the quality of the movies?

Drive-ins were never intended for cinema buffs. The sound systems were pathetic, your line of vision was obscured by passing cars, skimming popcorn boxes, and distressed-looking patrons looking for the washrooms — not to mention the welter of bug carcasses ossifying on your windshield.

But as I say, very few folks went to the drive-in to see the movie.

And no, madame, we didn't just go for *that*, either. Sure, the drive-ins had a seamy rep. "Passion pits," my father called them. I won't pretend that they were playing Trivial Pursuit in that '57

Chevy with the fogged-up windows in the back row, but there were a lot of kids in a lot of cars who weren't into any sexual hanky-panky.

They were just fantasizing about it.

Fact is, most of the high-school kids I knew (including your obedient scribbler) were dateless on a Saturday night, more often than not. We went to the drive-in anyway. Loading up on junk food, laughing at the terrible movies, and letting rip with megadecibel wolf whistles whenever we spotted a car in which the heads had disappeared from view.

I tell ya, there's no substitute for young sophistication.

But randy teenagers were not the only drive-in regulars. A lot of the incoming vehicles featured Mom and Dad up front, closely followed by a backseat full of hyperventilating kids, from adolescent down to toddler. Drive-ins were a swell recreational deal for young parents low on cash. Where else could you find a place that would feed you, entertain you, and allow you to fall asleep if you felt like it?

Plus, you could get in wearing pyjamas.

Such a good idea, the drive-in, and now they're almost as scarce as pterodactyl eggs. Why? What killed the drive-in?

A couple of things, I think. The price of land for starters. Any drive-in worth the price of admission has got to have at least five clear acres of parking.

Any idea how many townhouses you can cram onto five acres?

Then we have the modern car. Back in the forties, fifties, and sixties, North American cars were big and roomy, with sofa-sized seats and enough in-cab space to stage a volleyball game. Today's cars look like attaché cases. They're cramped and unyielding. Only a masochist would willingly spend an evening in them.

So the drive-in screens are going blank, one after another. On October 20, 1991, it was the turn of the K-W Drive-In in Kitchener, Ontario. The K-W's been packing them in Friday and Saturday nights for the past forty-one years. On the last night, just seventeen carloads paid to see *Forbidden Planet*, the last film that would ever flicker across the K-W's concrete block screen. The site has been sold to — here's a surprise — a land developer.

Forbidden Planet was pretty bad, even as lousy sci-fi thrillers go. But I'll betcha it's infinitely better than the next thing that pops up where the K-W Drive-In used to be.

Walk a Mall in My Shoes

THE ANCIENT GREEKS had the agora. The ancient Romans had the forum. In Spain, people still take an after-dinner ramble around the plaza, while in Italy, people wave and chat and sip their cappuccinos in the piazza. In modern Britain, people can yet get together to mix and mingle and murmur in gathering spots that range from the dinkiest village common to the hurly burly of Trafalgar Square. And here in Canada? What do we have here in Canada to compare to the agoras, the forums, the greens and commons and squares of the Old World?

Well, we have the Mall.

The shopping mall.

Kinda depressing as architectural wonders of the world go. The mall is to a village common as AstroTurf is to baseball: no matter how green and natural they try to make it, it still looks plastic.

The English poet Rupert Brooke described Canadian cities as consisting chiefly of banks and churches. That was a pre–World War One assessment. Today, the churches have pretty well faded into the background and the bank branch is usually buried in the glittery innards of a shopping mall, somewhere between Radio Shack and BJ's Den for Men. They're every-where, the malls. Any hamlet worthy of its "Welcome To" billboard sports at least a strip mall on the outskirts. Most towns of any size have entire mini-cities. They take up about the same acreage as a decent dairy farm.

Malls are not the same as village greens. They have a different purpose. Village greens are where folks go to relax. Malls are where you go to spend money.

At least, that's the way it's supposed to work. But I've got a feeling malls are changing.

Exhibit A: Scarborough Town Centre, early morning, any weekday, winter and summer. What do you find?

Not much business — the stores don't open for another two hours — but what's this? It looks like an army on the march. Platoon after platoon of mostly mature folks trudging steadfastly over the terrazzo, across one corridor, through the next, past the darkened stores, up stairs and down cul-de-sacs.

It's the Walk a Mall brigade. About two hundred of them, senior citizens for the most part, show up at 7:30 a.m., Monday to Friday. They hike the mall for two hours. And they pay for the privilege. Not much, mind you — dues are only five dollars annually. Quite a bargain when you consider that the mall owners and merchants kick in $10,000 a year. The money goes for health seminars, snacks, parking, coat check, and club T-shirts. The Scarborough mall is just one of dozens across the country hosting this new breed of non-shopping visitor. The Walk a Mall idea is spreading — as well it might in a country where city walking is arduous at best and downright hazardous at times.

What's in it for the malls? Great PR. As for the mall marchers, it's a healthy habit and an easy, natural way to make new friends.

And you know, if you just kind of squint your eyes as you're huffing and puffing past the potted palms, right by the Tropic Tan booth there . . . why, you'd almost think you were walking through a Barcelona plaza.

Anybody Bring a Flashlight?

I T'S A STRANGELY PEACEFUL feeling, being in a cave. Eerie, for sure, but undeniably peaceful. Well, not so strange, I guess, when you think of it. Humans have put in several thousand more years crouching in caves than we have relaxing in condos. And we all spend our first nine months in the warmest, darkest, safest cave we'll ever experience.

It's nice to know they're still there, caves. Under our feet. Up along the ridge. Just in case we, you know, should ever need them again. Heck, they're there, all right. This planet is honeycombed with caves. There are limestone caves, lava caves, ice caves, sea caves. Castleguard, the longest cave in Canada, stretches for more than 12 miles under Banff National Park — but that's a driveway culvert compared with the longest known cave system in the world. Mammoth Cave Park, in Kentucky, winds and intersects for more than 340 pitch-black miles.

Some caves are potholes, some of them are deep. There's one in France called the Gouffre Jean Bernard, which a crack team of cavers decided to get to the bottom of a few years ago. They gave up at 5,256 feet . . . just eight yards short of a mile straight down. There was still plenty of dark beneath them.

Some caves are, well, cavernous. Carlsbad Cavern in New Mexico, the bat caves of Texas. There's a cave in Gibraltar that houses a natural amphitheatre big enough to accommodate an orchestra, a chorus, and a large audience. Great acoustics. But that's still pretty piddly compared with the granddaddy of them all — Sarawak Chamber in Malaysia. Sarawak Chamber is 2,300 feet long, averages 980 feet across, and is nowhere less than the height of a fifteen-storey building. Someone with a lot of time on his or her hands has figured out that the Sarawak Chamber is commodious enough to accommodate ten jumbo jets lined up nose cone to tailfin, thirty-eight football fields, or 7,500 buses.

Though not all at once.

Of course, caves also run to the other extreme. I know of one Blue Mountain cave that contains a passage called Fat Man's Misery. The instructions for getting yourself through this little Precambrian sphincter run something along the lines of "place your right arm straight over your head and your left arm down along your left side. Lift your right knee up and place your right foot on the ledge. Now let all the air out of your lungs and push forward . . ."

No, thanks. I never did make it to the other side of Fat Man's Misery.

It's not that I'm . . . that fat. I don't think I'm even a closet claustrophobe. It was just a little too dark and a little too dank with a little too much tonnage of cold, merciless granite pressing in from all sides.

It was a personal moment of truth for me. The truth I discovered is that I am not a spelunker.

Funny word, eh? "Spelunk." I spelunk. You spelunk.

They tell me it comes from the Latin word for cave. But I prefer to think it comes from the depths of the earth itself. I like to imagine spelunking is what happens to the skinnier, foolhardier cavers who brushed by me to shimmy disdainfully through Fat Man's Misery, only to discover too late the slippery thousand-foot precipice on the other side. Spelunking is the reward we chubbier, more sensible folk get to hear, floating up through the inky subterranean void.

Sounds like AAAAAAAaaaaaaaaaaaaaaaaaaaaaaaaaaaa . . .

Spe LUNK!

The Barbie Summit

THE PHOENICIANS LEFT US MONEY. The ancient Greeks bequeathed democracy. The Romans created the basis of the law we still use today. The Arabs begat algebra and so with the Germans, French, Spanish, Italians — philosophy, sculpture, music, poetry. What if . . . what if after all of the hype and hoopla of the twentieth century expires . . . what if the greatest legacy America left the planet was . . .

The Barbie doll.

Think about it. America has spawned no Socratic-calibre philosophers. Composers? How many John Cages would you take for a Beethoven sonata? Could Andy Warhol clean Picasso's brushes? Is there a Milton in the house?

Ah, but dolls. Now. America takes a backseat in the baby carriage to no one when it comes to dolls. And there has never in the history of the world been a doll like Barbie. She's thirty-something but doesn't look a polymer older than the day she was extruded, back in 1958.

Her secret? Adaptability. Let Darwinian determinism do its damnedest, Barbie rides the wave of change. She was a debutante in the fifties, a free spirit in the sixties, a preppie in the seventies, and — wiff! — a little backcomb, a designer briefcase, and a headband . . . a yuppy in the eighties. Now, striding personfully through the wind-down decade of the century, has the march of time finally caught Barbie in the stretch?

Not on your burgundy BMW. Barbie is ready. Barbie is poised

to host just the cutest little world peace summit your kids ever lusted after.

It's all in a press release from Mattel Toys. The city of New York was chosen as the venue for a Barbie Peace Summit. Children with Barbies from all over the world (I'm not making this up) convened in New York (seriously now) to voice their opinions (are you sitting down?) on changing the world. And Mattel, just in the spirit of planetary humanitarianism, you understand, and by utter coincidence, released an all-new line of four ethnic dolls as symbols of this summit. Four ecumenical mannequins I dare say every Barbie lover will have to add to her or his collection.

Mattel's not in this for the money. As a matter of fact, the company lashed out a few grand to fly a six-year-old East Berliner to New York, just for a press conference.

"When the Berlin Wall came down," says the Mattel press release, little Anika Polzin "was finally able to fulfill her hope of owning the doll that inspires many of her fantasies."

ALL RIGHT!! The collapse of global communism means Anika can now buy that Barbie workout wardrobe that Soviet serfs used to read about in samizdat flyers passed furtively hand to hand. The workout wardrobe, the exercise station, and maybe . . . maybe Anika's village could band together, pool their Deutsche Marks, and purchase a communal Ken doll too. And ain't that what democracy's all about?

Exciting concept, the Barbie Summit. Mind you, there are still one or two details to nail down. Such as, what will Barbie wear? No doubt Mattel will think of something. And if there's any justice at all in this changing world, the keynote address at the Barbie Summit will be delivered by America's living Ken doll, Dan Quayle. It's not as if he's busy these days.

Don't Look Now, But This Country's Bugged

And the black-flies, the little black-flies,
Always the black-fly no matter where you go,
I'll die with the black-fly apickin' my bones
In North Ontario-io
                    — venerable Canadian song lyric

WE'RE ON THE DOWNSLIDE side of another summer, no question about it — but that's not so bad for humans. The approach of autumn means no more than an extra blanket on the bed for you and me. It's the kiss of death for bugs.

Yep, all those nasty little critters with stingers and buzzers and feelers and altogether too many legs are just one hard frost away from meeting their maker. I am not a bloodthirsty man, but the thought of billions of man-eating bugs clutching their hearts and falling flat on their carapaced backs fill me with joy unalloyed. *DIE, you little #*@*#&'s!* I'm delighted to know that I'll never see you again, and so is the back of my neck.

If there is a heaven, and if I ever get there, I hope there's a Question Period. I can't wait to ask the Chief Product Control Officer why he or she thought a planet (already infested with a surfeit of lawyers, politicians, and the incipient threat of haemorrhoids) needed such a bewildering variety of insects with a taste for human pelt.

Because it isn't just black-flies that want to jump our veins. It's mosquitoes and deer flies and horseflies and mites and gnats and beer bugs and noseeums — all, all of the vampiric persuasion.

151

And in some parts of this country — everything north of Tecumseh Road in Windsor, Ontario — they hover in clouds, nay, *galaxies* just waiting for some fat, pink, warm-blooded creature in bermuda shorts to blunder by.

Why so many of them? And what do they do for lunch when they don't have my body to fight over for drilling rights?

I can't prove it, but I suspect if you peeled back the lichens that blanket the floor of Canada's boreal forest, you'd find countless tiny, gothic, Frankensteinian castles each no bigger than a good-sized mosquito welt. And I bet if you could peer into the darkest vault in the miniature dungeons beneath each of those castles, you'd see row after row of eensy-weensy coffins lining the walls.

That's where the bugs live. In those coffins. Just imagine 80 kazillion dwarf Bela Lugosis wearing deely boppers. Until I, like a fool, show up for a camping trip or a barbecue. That's when the bug lookout rings the dinner gong, 80 kazillion tiny coffin lids slide back, and the bugs come after me, buzzing their blood-curdling battle cry: "*Soup's onnnnnnnnn!*"

It's not that grim everywhere in Canada, of course. Insect intensity varies greatly across our Dominion. The mosquitoes that wait in ambush along the shores of Ungava Bay, for instance, are the Exocet missiles of the biting bug world. They make mosquitoes that live and prey along the American border look like limp-mandibled pantywaists. Folks in Vancouver, on the other hand, love to skinny-dip in their hot tubs out on the deck, airily remarking that they "have no mosquitoes to worry about."

Yeah, well, they got Bill Vander Zalm too. Everything evens out.

In any case, it could be worse. We Canucks could be living in Equatorial Africa, watching a Goliath beetle trying to Have His Way with the family Volkswagen in the driveway. Goliath beetles are as big as your hand, tipping the scales at nearly a quarter of a pound.

And I've heard tell of a water-dwelling insect that inhabits certain South American rivers. In between hosts, that is. This critter prefers to live in the urinary tracts of mammals dumb enough to urinate in the river. The bug is extremely heat-sensitive, and small enough to home in on and swim up the urinary tract of larger animals, including humans. The bug lodges in the urinary tract, using spiny fins that open up like an umbrella to keep him there.

The pain, I am told, is in livid Technicolor.

On second thought, Canadian bugs don't seem half bad.

Down Home

WENT DOWN HOME last week. Well, the Maritimes. It's not my home, but that's what my expatriate Maritime friends call it when they go back to Musquodoboit or Anapolis Valley or Moncton. They say they're going Down Home. And that's what it feels like when you go there, even if you were born and raised somewhere else entirely. Harry Bruce, a born-again Maritimer and a fine writer, said it best. "If a Maritimer," wrote Harry, "says 'Down Home' while sitting in a Toronto tavern, he could be talking about all the Maritimes, or Prince Edward Island, or a valley, cove, county, village, or the house where he grew up."

Well, when I say "Down Home" I'm talking about a down-and-dirty, smash-and-grab, sign-and-smile literary blitz of bookstores, radio studios, and television yak fests in Fredericton, Halifax, and Charlottetown. Three Down Home cities in three days. The idea is to sell as many people as you can on the idea of picking up a copy of your brand-new book.

Such a sortie subjects a body to more restaurant meals, luggage carousels, and impregnable motel shampoo packets than is good for one. But there's an up side. You're Down Home.

The realization that you are not within the dread tractor beam of Toronto comes to you in funny ways. Cars Down Home actually *stop* to let you cross the street in front of them — without a stoplight or a crossing guard or a pedestrian walkway, mind. The Halifax Air Canada agent who escorts you off the airplane on

Tuesday night is there to greet you when you fly out on Wednesday — and he remembers your name. Of course, maybe the awkward bundle you've got under your arm jogs his memory. It's a split-cane three-piece fishing rod held together with twist ties. "Gonna do a little fly fishing in Charlottetown, are you, Mr. Black?" he inquires with just a hint of a chiding smile. There's snow on the ground and ice on the rivers, but you know these tourists. You explain that the fishing rod is a gift. From a wonderful old gent in a Scottish tam who showed up at a Fredericton radio station and insisted the visitor take the rod. "It's an antique," explained the old gent, "just like me. I want you to have it. You've given me lots of pleasure on the air, I want to give you some on the water."

As a broadcaster I've received T-shirts and baseball caps and one time somebody gave me a half pound of peanut brittle, but this is my very first antique split-cane bamboo fly fishing rod. Fitting that it should happen Down Home.

Down Home taxis are different too. In Toronto, cabs are emblazoned with No Smoking injunctions. My cab driver in Halifax offers me a cigarette. Then asks if I mind if he smokes. Well, normally, yes . . . but this is Down Home. After most Toronto cab rides I feel about as close to the driver as I do to the vehicle's fan belt, but on the cab ride from the Fredericton airport, the driver brings me up to date on New Brunswick weather (fine for the last month), his kids (one boy and one girl), his past (navy, twenty-three years), and his perception of the federal government (censored). He takes my money at the hotel door, carries my bags to the desk, wishes me a good stay, and disappears with an easy, Down Home wave.

And the next morning when I'm checking out (here's the real Down Home part), the desk clerk presents me with a big white taxi driver's envelope. On the envelope I read: "Mr. Black: You paid me 16 dollars for airport run, but when I passed my charges in, I realized that your fare was prepaid. I got paid twice. That is nice but what is yours is yours. Within is sixteen dollars. Have a good breakfast. Signed Duncan, Car number three."

Well thanks, Duncan, but if it's all right with you, I have a better idea. When the show's over I'm going to take the "Basic Black" crew out for a Down Home salute.

Waiter? Beers all around. Moosehead, of course.

Don't Mess with My Throne

For a man's house is his castle, et domus sua cuique tutissimum refugium.

AN ENGLISH JURIST by the name of Sir Edward Coke wrote that, way back in Shakespeare's time.

A man's home is his castle. It is the very foundation of British common law. It means that, while our governments may lie to us, while they may cheat us and tax us and spend our money foolishly and send our children off to fight their stupid wars, our governments cannot, by God, jerk us around in our own living rooms.

Because a man's home is his castle.

And if the domestic castle is sacred ground, is there a chamber within that's holier than that one tiny room, perhaps the last place in the fortress where a man or a woman can be assured of a few minute's privacy?

They don't call it the Throne Room for nothing, you know.

I love my bathroom for just that reason. It's my refuge. The one place in the house where, for a short while at least, I can legitimately be excused from taking phone calls, feeding the dog, or pretending I have a clue about my kid's algebra assignment.

'Twas ever thus. I don't have actual data, but I'm reasonably certain that folks down through the ages have always retired to their respective privies when the urge for solitude came upon them.

Which makes me wonder where the next generation is going to go for a little peace and quiet.

As a retreat, the bathroom is an endangered species. My newspaper tells me that the Trendy Folk down in California are

157

retrofitting their bathrooms with — are you ready for this? — home computers, fax machines, and cordless telephones.

David Shapiro is a chap in Van Nuys, California, who makes a living remodelling other people's bathrooms. And a very good living it is. Shapiro says that some of his clients are spending upwards of $100,000 to outfit their water closets as "social areas."

If you're thinking that it might be a little cramped wedging a Xerox machine in between the toilet and the bathroom weigh scales, I'm with you. But Californians (the ones with money, at least) think bigger than you and I do. Any resemblance between their bathroom and the ones you and I hang out in is utterly coincidental.

According to David Shapiro, his customers are punching out the walls and raising roofbeams in their washrooms so that the new "spaces" can accommodate easychairs, sofas, and even gym equipment.

The idea, says Shapiro, is to make the bathroom more accessible so that "kids can come in and talk while their parents are getting ready for work or doing their exercise routines."

Is it just me or is this the most grotesque idea to come down the California Turnpike since Roseanne?

I don't know about you, but I don't wish to talk to my kids when I'm "getting ready for work" in my bathroom. We can debate the meaning of existence over the Wheaties in the kitchen. I'll be delighted to handle any teenage queries in the living room, the basement, or even the attic.

But when it comes to the bathroom, one at a time, please.

As for the idea of turning my bathroom into a work station with fax machines, cordless phones, and a colour-coordinated Tandy laptop, I recall that Hugh Hefner, the Playboy poohbah, had a sign over the door of his Chicago pad that read: "If You Don't Swing, Don't Ring."

I'm thinking of installing a brass plaque over my bathroom door. It will read: "If You Ring (or Buzz or Hum or Boot or Click or Make Copies), Stay the Hell Out of My Bathroom!"

Banner Occasions

DESERT STORM HAS COME and long gone now, leaving many bizarre images tattooed on the collective human brainpan. One of the most bizarre for me is one I saw on TV long after the bombing runs had stopped and the troops had left the Persian Gulf. It was the week of the great Desert Storm welcome-home victory parades across the U.S. On CNN, they showed a whole cavalcade of Desert Stormers — soldiers, sailors, airmen, and their hardware — strutting down the streets of Boston. They were preceded by a flotilla of prancing majorettes. Majorettes dressed in skimpy bikinis. Bikinis consisting solely of red, white, and blue stars and stripes. The American flag, writ exceedingly small.

Ah, yes. The flag thing, as George Bush might have said. Strange, the various reactions a little swatch of bunting can generate south of the border. While hapless hippies rot their lives away in Texas jails for daring to set fire to the flag, patriotic Boston majorettes get to wear Old Glory as a bra and panty set.

Here in Canada we don't have that kind of ferocious, schizoid fascination with our flag. Americans can't even talk about Old Glory without getting a Walter Cronkite warble in their voice. Canadians murmur diffidently about "the, um, Maple Leaf."

And we don't flash our flag around like the Americans do. They fly it from their gas stations, their corner stores, their mailboxes, their biceps. Canucks don't flaunt the flag like that.

As a matter of fact, we can't. It's against the law. Here in Canada we have rules about where you can and can't fly your flag. As a resort in Banff, Alberta, learned, when they got an official letter from the secretary of state ordering them to stop flying the Maple Leaf, as it were. The company has a tourist brochure that shows a teensy-weensy Canadian flag up in the top right-hand corner. "Violation! Violation!" shrilled the Ottawa Thought Police. The company brochure can't show the flag because the company didn't *ask Ottawa's permission* to show the flag.

Despite protests that the flag already appears on everything from Team Canada sweatshirts to Johnny on the Spot outhouses, Ottawa was unmoved. "The fact that it's done by thousands of businesses," harrumphed a government spokesman, "doesn't make it right."

Fortunately, things aren't wrong just because some government flunky says they are. The Banff company told Ottawa to take a hike, and so did Joe Jansen, the head of the Banff–Lake Louise Chamber of Commerce. "You've got Joe Clark running around trying to keep the country together," fumed Jansen, "and some other guy in Ottawa telling us not to use the flag."

Matter of fact, there was such a backlash that within the week Ottawa issued a hasty apology, declaring that "in this case" it would be all right for the company to show the flag on its brochure.

The government spokesman said Ottawa was merely concerned that the appearance of the flag on advertising might make people think the government supported the goods or services being promoted.

I think they worry unduly. I think the public knows the difference between the Canadian flag and the folks who currently live on the top floor of the Ottawa sandcastle. The flag is ours, not the government's. We intend to keep the flag. As for the government, well . . . we'll all have something to say about that come election day.

Uncle Sam
Wants Us

I SEE L. CRAIG SCHOONMAKER is in the news again. Mr. Schoonmaker is a modest eccentric who dwells in a shabby apartment in midtown Manhattan, cranking out press releases for his Expansionist Party. The Expansionist Party has but one knot-holed plank in its rickety platform — it would like to make Canada the fifty-first state. Or states. L. Craig Schoonmaker is not an unreasonable man. He thinks, given Canada's size and natural wealth, we might even rate two or three state status.

Well, L. Craig Schoonmaker would be to laugh if it weren't for other signs you see around. Big signs, like disappearing rail services and self-erasing international borders. And little signs, like CTV's Sunday schedule and Alice Munro's dustjacket copy.

Ms. Munro, of Clinton, Ontario, is one of the best writers this country has ever produced. But Random House, the American publisher that controls her U.S. rights, thinks merely being Canada's best might not give her books that needed nudge in the bookstores.

So Random House has amended reality.

On the dustjacket of her recent short-story collection they describe Alice Munro as "one of America's leading writers of short fiction."

That doesn't bother me. We're used to the inclusive all-American bear hug our cousins dish out whenever they run into somebody who's white and dresses like they might hail from Iowa. What bothers me is the way the Random House apologist explained away the gaffe. Calling her an American, said the Random House flack, was, quote, "meant respectfully. She was described that way because she is highly regarded around the world." Unquote.

Oh yeah, sure, right, I see your point. Would never have done to describe her as a Canadian.

Then there's CTV and its flagship current affairs show, "W5." Perhaps more lifeboat dinghy than flagship, actually. We found out how important some CTV execs think "W5" is when they bumped it out of its regular prime-time slot with less than a week's notice to make room for . . . "America's Funniest Home Videos." "W5" is a first-rate show, but it *is* about Canada and does require viewers to, you know, *think*. Unlike "America's Funniest Home Videos."

It's getting harder and harder to just be a Canadian, isn't it? Bad enough dealing with the dizzy sister next door flying into a tantrum every couple of weeks and snatching for the car keys. On top of that you've got crinkle-eyed Sam, our rich uncle from down south with the gold bicuspid and the smile that never quite fades. Always trying the doors and rattling the windows. Says he just wants us to sit on his knee, but Mom warned us about guys like him . . .

How do you keep a canoe upright in tricky water like that? Dalton Camp says you do it by being realistic. "Be realistic about Canada," he once wrote. "We are a minority shareholder and we have the inevitable options of the minority shareholder — the limited powers of persuasion and the unfathomable powers of prayer."

Mmmmm. How's that old Cornish prayer go? "From ghoulies and ghosties and long-leggety beasties, good Lord, deliver us!"

Yeah, and you can throw in L. Craig Schoonmaker and the guy in the stovepipe hat, too.

Joyful Sex: The Canadian Position

THE JAPANESE PERUSED pillow books. The Indians studied the Kama Sutra. The Italians learned their lessons from *The Decameron*. The French took their cue from the memoirs of Casanova. And North Americans? North Americans got the *Joy of Sex*. Kind of a *Fanny Hill* as told to Mr. Rogers.

I suppose just about every North American over the age of thirty-five bought, borrowed, or at least thumbed through *The Joy of Sex* back in the early seventies. You know the one, the Gourmet Guide to Lovemaking, Complete and Unabridged, Illustrated Edition, compiled by the serendipitously named Alex Comfort, MB, PhD.

Well, no rest for the wicked, I guess. Dr. Comfort, that randy old rake, has risen to the occasion once more. Now at bookstores everywhere: *JoySex III* — or to give it its proper title: *The New Joy of Sex: A Gourmet Guide to Lovemaking in the Nineties.*

What's new about sex twenty years later? A king Hell sandtrap called AIDS, for one thing. Gotta give Dr. Comfort a few strokes off for daring to bring out a sex manual in an era when a lot of would-be swingers are Just Saying No . . . Thanks.

But *The New Joy of Sex* is nothing if not à la mode. It's even pinched a soupçon of the nationalistic fervour currently sweeping the planet. Poles, Czechs, Albanians, and Latvians demanding their own space? Then, by Eros, the least Doc Comfort can do is make sure they have their own sexual positions to occupy those spaces. Thus in *The New Joy of*, we discover acrobatic configurations that even a gymnast like Nadia Comaneci, never mind a cosmopolitan contortionist like Casanova, never dreamed of. The book gives us intimate, full-colour delineation and description of the Indian and Japanese preferred positions. We can also peruse at leisure the Serbian Stance, the Croatian Crouch, and the Hungarian Huddle. Not to mention the lyrical Chinese, who seem to ride a sexual seesaw between Wailing Monkey Clasping Tree and Wild Geese Flying on Their Backs.

There is one glaring omission from *The New Joy of Sex*. I can find nary a line drawing nor rhyming couplet that deals with the Canadian Coital Question. What's the preferred posture here in the Great White North? Bellowing Moose with Trembling Aspen? Shivering Beaver Under Soaring Eagle? Not a jot or a tittle about it in this book.

Never mind the position, what about the romantic setting for Canuck-style cuddling? A loaf of prairie bannock, a jug of Niagara wine, and thou beside me, singing sea shanties in the barren lands? Too predictable.

But dammit all, this is an important question — and one that needs to be answered before Dr. Comfort hits us with *Son of All New More Joy of Sex Four, the Sequel*. The Canadian position — and location — need to be defined!

I know! We'll handle it the Canadian way. First we'll appoint a Royal Commission . . . and then we'll ask Quebec!

When Ya Gotta Go . . .

It's not that I'm afraid to die. I just don't want to be there when it happens.

— Woody Allen

A H, YES. DEATH. The final taboo. Go into a bar, slip onto a barstool, strike up a conversation with the person next to you, and chances are pretty good that before you're halfway through your first sasparilla, you'll hear more about his or her political beliefs, religious convictions, and sexual orientation than you ever wanted to know.

But if you ask the stranger about death? Zipper lips. Clam city. And a sidelong we-don't-allow-weirdos-in-here glare from the suddenly chilly bartender.

We're a civilization of inveterate gabbers — except when the subject is death.

Which is a pity, considering it's an appointment we all have to keep.

Of course, some exits are more spectacular than others. Joan of Arc went out, quite literally, in a blaze of glory, incinerated by the Church as a heretic. Zeuxis the Greek, on the other hand, underwent a more ignominious finale. Zeuxis, a painter who lived around 500 B.C., daubed a satirical portrait of an old woman that made him laugh so hard he blew a blood vessel in his head and died on the spot.

Death can be, as someone once said, like a pie in the face from God. Take the case of Allan Pinkerton. You would think the founder of the world-famous Pinkerton's detective agency would go out in a hail of gunfire or at the very least on silken sheets attended by the best physicians money could rent. Not so. Mr. P. stumbled one morning while taking his morning constitutional, biting his tongue. The wound turned gangrenous and Mr. Pinkerton died.

Or consider Claudius I. One would expect such an august personage to expire with all the pomp and majesty befitting a numero uno in the Roman Empire. Uh-uh. Claudius choked on a chicken feather — a chicken feather that, ironically, his personal physician had thrust down the Emperor's throat to induce vomiting. (Claudius's wife, it seems, had been slipping her hubby poisoned mushrooms in an attempt to become sole custodian of the family jewels.)

Indeed, in the game of death, Irony often lays it on thick and heavy. I don't know if curiosity killed the cat, but it certainly didn't do Sir Francis Bacon any favours. Riding through a snowstorm in his carriage one day, Sir Francis had a brainwave that stuffing dead bodies with snow might slow down decay. He stopped his carriage, got out and purchased a chicken, killed it on the spot, and stuffed it with snow.

Alas, Sir Francis never got to write up the experiment. He caught a chill from his chicken-buying spree, which turned into a fatal bout of pneumonia.

The award for Most Grotesque Death goes to Thomas May, a seventeenth-century English historian. Mr. May was fat. Very fat. So fat he had double chins on his double chins. May's pendulous jowls got to be such a logistical problem that he took to tying them up with bandannas. While shovelling down dinner one day, Mr. May began to hiccup. By the time bystanders got his throat kerchiefs untied, he'd choked to death.

Let us close the coffin lid on this grisly chapter with the story of Yousuf Ishmaelo, a world-champion Turkish wrestler who toured North America in the late nineteenth century, defeating all comers and amassing a fortune — which he converted into gold coins and kept in a leather pouch that he wore day and night.

What safer place? The man was a mountain of muscle. Who could take it from him?

Well, an old mat mama who fights under the name of Mother Nature, actually. Yousuf and his money belt went down with his ship off Nova Scotia. He could easily have swum to safety, you understand — but not with a belt full of gold around his waist. And Yousuf stubbornly refused to part with his leather pouch right to the end.

Which is not a fate I'll ever have to worry about.

My wallet's so empty I could use it for flotation.

Bizarre Burials

BENJAMIN FRANKLIN SAID, "In this world nothing is certain but death and taxes." Ben Franklin was too optimistic by half. We can only count on taxes from here on in. Death has had its stinger plucked. You can no longer end it all by dying. They'll only dig you right back up again.

Take the case of poor Zachary Taylor, a modestly talented old war horse catapulted into the Oval Office in 1849, where he did little enough damage until expiring not quite a year and a half later.

A quiet, uneventful presidency. No hollow walking sticks full of bourbon, no Mafiosa bimbettes under the White House eiderdown. No Nixonian burglaries, no Reaganite arms deals with terrorists. Zachary Taylor was clean. You'd think they could leave a chap like that alone, once they'd tamped the earth down?

Not a chance. They dug old Zachary up not long ago, put him on a slab, and turned a couple of forensic ferrets loose on him. Why? A historian thought maybe he'd been poisoned. She was wrong. But even if she'd been right, would it have mattered? To the *National Enquirer,* sure . . . but to poor old Zack, his heirs and assigns? I think not. Let's face it — the only positive side to croaking is that you do get that great nap. If they're gonna start popping coffin lids like beer caps, there'd be no point in dying at all.

And it looks like it may become a trend. There's talk of exhuming President Lincoln's remains to check for Marfan's disease. Who, not counting Marfan, cares? What next?

Maybe they'll want to dig up Sandra West. She's been six feet under in a San Antonio grave since 1977. In her negligée. Sitting up. In the seat. Of her Ferrari. Yes, her Ferrari. A blue one. But easy with the pickaxes. The grave is wired to discourage upwardly mobile ghouls.

Or they might try tapping on the sod above Ontario's own Aimee Semple McPherson. Aimee was a whooping, wailing, evangelical sin-buster — kind of a flapper version of Tammy Faye Bakker. Aimee went through several careers, fortunes, and husbands before dying in Oakland, California, in 1944. She's buried there. They could dig her up. Or just call her up. Aimee's will stipulated that a working telephone be installed in her coffin. Nobody's ever called, of course. Scared to, I guess. What if you got a busy signal?

Death and taxes. Death and taxes. Let me leave you with a story about death and actors. Happened at the funeral of Maurice Barrymore, famous actor and father of actors John, Lionel, and Ethel. As they were lowering the coffin into the grave, one of the straps twisted. The coffin had to be raised again for adjustment. Observing the box coming out of the ground, Lionel rolled his eyes and in his best stage whisper rumbled, "How like father — a curtain call."

PART 5

The Other Crew Members on Spaceship Earth

Rufus: The Columnist's Friend

"DEAR ARTHUR: I LOVE YOUR COLUMN! It's the first thing I read when I pick up the paper. But I'm curious — surely it doesn't take you seven whole days to fill half a page of newsprint. What do you do the rest of the week?

"Signed: Faithful reader in Richmond."

Well, Faithful (can I call you Faith?), you're right. It doesn't take seven whole days to write a column. Some weeks I find myself with whole spare minutes on my hands. Much of it I spend as I'm sure you do — letting in the cat and putting out the garbage, subduing dandelions on my front lawn, broken-heartedly weeding strands out of my hairbrush and wondering if I should take up crocheting toupees.

But mostly, Faith, old pal, mostly I spend my spare time doing what I'm doing right now — sitting here, staring at the mute, accusatorial, phosphorescent glow of a blank computer screen, waiting for inspiration to strike.

Sometimes, when it's very close to deadline (as it is now), I pray a little.

"I'm not asking for the Great Canadian Novel, Lord," I'll say. "Just a little notion, you know, something that could maybe fill a half page of a newspaper."

I look out my window. Nope. Wrote about looking out my window last month.

Hum a few bars of "Get a Job." Glance at calendar on wall.

Study fingernails. (Hangnails. Have I ever written about hangnails? Probably.)

Despairingly look down at feet.

And there it is. My inspiration. Rufus the Wonderdog. My stalwart furred amigo and staunch four-pawed companion! A last-minute desperation move? Not a bit of it. Rufus is a dog worthy of a whole series of columns — if not a feature-length documentary. Okay, you're not seeing him at his best right now, collapsed over my bedroom slippers, snoring with his tongue hanging out. But at least you can see his basic features. Colour: black and white, just like a Holstein (and at 85 pounds, built kinda like a Holstein, minus the horns and udder). Breed: Australian shepherd — or so the pet store owner seemed to mutter out of the corner of his mouth while he was counting my money.

I take it on faith that he's terrific at shepherding Australians, because he's certainly good for nothing else.

Well, not true. In times of crisis, Rufus responds like a trained member of a crack Canine Commando Corps. A knock on the door, an explosion, a raised voice, a low-flying bluebottle — Rufus's response is instantaneous and unquestioning. He growls, barks, then gallops directly to his owner (me) and sits on my chest.

Worse luck for me if I happen to be standing.

Other attributes? Rufus hates squirrels (though not enough to actually, you know, *confront* one) and has deep misgivings about any human being under the height of 36 inches. Though not precisely a coward, Rufus will never be confused with Don Cherry's bull terrier (or with Don Cherry, come to that). He's a nonfighter. A pacifist. If he barked with a lisp, I'd solder a bowtie to his collar and name him Lester B.

He has other talents that are less endearing.

He's the only dog I know who howls when he hears the National Research Council's official time signal.

He's the only dog I know who passes gas at the sound of Kim Campbell's voice.

Which is why we don't watch the news much around our place.

Rufus is not what you'd call gainfully employed. In fact, if the deadbeats of the world ever need a mascot, I would nominate my mutt to stand (lie) for office.

But he's cute and he loves to lick you right in the face when you need it most — and once, his sham, preposterous John Crosbie bark actually drove a flock of pesky Jehovah's Witnesses from my door.

And then of course there's the time he shuffled into my office, collapsed on my carpet slippers, looked up at me with those big Uncle Tom brown eyes . . .

And saved my bacon, thirty minutes before my deadline.

Flossed the Dog Lately?

L OOKING FOR A LITTLE sparkle in the gloom, are you? A little champagne among the bubbles? A snatch of pizzicato in the ongoing dirge? Sick to death of hearing about floods and blights and droughts and new tax incentives? Are you up for a little Good News?

Well, I've got good news for you. Gleaned from the pages of *Good Dog!* I swear, *Good Dog!*, magazine. This is a periodical published quarterly and lovingly dedicated to the care and feeding of man's best friend. The good news is: you don't have to worry about flossing your dog's teeth.

It's here on page 13, see? Veterinary dentist Peter Emily writes: "People [that's you and me] have tight spaces between their teeth. Debris and plaque get caught in there . . . Dogs only have two small areas where the teeth are in contact like this . . . As I see it," writes the vet dentist, "flossing a dog's teeth is unnecessary. Brushing in a circular motion will take care of it."

Is that not great news? Doesn't that pluck a whopper of a burden from your care-stooped shoulders? I'm relieved. I think. Although, as I ponder it, small nagging worries begin to raise their tiny, cranky, Corgi-like heads.

Circular brushing, huh? My dog? It opens up a whole new field of hygiene paranoia. What's next — Odorono Paw Pads? Fur gel? What about breath fresheners — there's a canine frontier for you! Can't you see the TV commercials? Head and shoulders close-ups of a Peke and a Pomeranian snout to snout, snarling, "Grrrts is a candy mint! Grrrts is a breath mint!"

Ooops! Too late! Right here on page 35 of the selfsame issue of *Good Dog!* magazine, an easy-to-make, environment-friendly home recipe to combat dreaded doggy breath: a concoction made of baking soda and . . . garlic? Why garlic? "Dogs like garlic," the article explains.

Which is fine, except that I don't, that much. Not when it's being chuffed out by a panting pooch in my parlour, anyway.

That's the trouble with progress: every breakthrough comes with its own dog's breakfast of new and unanticipated headaches.

This idea of brushing a dog's teeth in a circular motion, for instance. Now take Don Cherry. He's about as tough a Canuck as has ever been fitted for a cup, but I've got a hunch Cherry could talk till he was Blue in the face and never convince his homely mutt about the virtues of oral preventive hygiene. And his is a gentle dog. I don't want to be around when some poor health-conscious pet owner attempts to ply a Picopay on a pit bull.

Worries, worries, worries. I'd like to stay and fret about it some more, but I have to go.

Gotta give my Australian shepherd a gum massage.

Mutts on the Workforce

I HAD HIGH HOPES that Great Britain was going to lighten up a little after Iron Maggie stepped down and that nice Mr. Major took over, but it appears not. London officialdom seems more retrenched and hardline than ever. The British House of Commons has formally voted to ban pet dogs from the Palace of Westminster. That decision unceremoniously turfs some seventeen canine companions who had been accustomed to spending their days at the feet of their government-employed human colleagues.

The usual rationales have been trotted out: dogs are unhygienic, noisy, a distraction. But I'm not fooled. This is pure bureaucratic curmudgeonism at work. Dogs in the workplace are the best thing that ever happened to a workplace, and anybody who doesn't think so is a cur.

I know. Years ago when I toiled in a quieter, more peaceful outpost of the CBC, I used to bring my old dog Angus to work every day.

He slept under my desk, cadged crusts from Miss Vicki the receptionist, licked the odd guest, and once yawned audibly, on the air, while I was reading the five-thirty news.

Well, it was a pretty boring newscast.

I think Angus enjoyed punching the CBC clock. I know I loved having him around and I believe most of the staff did too. Although the news editor was distinctly cool.

But then Angus up and died and I up and moved, and more important, a three-alarm now-read-this CBC memo appeared one day on bulletin boards of CBC stations across the nation. Due to concern about hygiene, noise, distraction, blah blah blah, dogs were henceforth banned from CBC premises. Rumour had it that it was Barbara Frum's lap grizzly that precipitated the memo. I don't know anything about that. All I know is in the halls of the CBC these days, you'll encounter more Tory Welcome Wagons than you will mutts.

And that's a shame. It's nice to be able to reach down and chuck a shaggy ally behind the ears from time to time. Nice to take a break once in a while to escort your pal on a constitutional around the block. Dr. Roger Mugford, a well-known animal behaviour consultant, says, "Dogs at work can become a nice focus for friendship formation and a good source of light-hearted tension relief." That's true. I can remember folks dropping into my office when Angus was around. They didn't want to see me. They wanted to interface with some personnel who wouldn't ask them about memos, expense accounts, or contributions to the Wayward Reporters Benevolent Fund. That was where Angus fitted in. No demands. Although if you happened to have a spare sandwich crust kicking around . . .

Dogs work in the office. Well, they don't work, but they fit in fine. Alas, it's very hard to convince your average office manager of that.

And on second thought, maybe it's better that way. Maybe it's more humane to leave dogs at home. I mean, with the telephone ringing and the fax machine screeching and computer terminals bip-bipping and everybody yacking at everybody else . . . it's a dog's life in here.

Come the Revolution...

*Heaven goes by favour. If it went by merit, you
would stay out and your dog would go in.*
— Mark Twain

OLD SAM CLEMENS WAS right, you know. It's a lucky thing we
humans wrote the Bible. It gave us a chance to make ourselves look good and to grab the captain's cabin on Spaceship
Earth. Ever since we put ourselves in charge of the planet, the way
we've treated our fellow tenants has been something less than
charitable.

When white men first came to this continent, the skies were
blackened by migrating passenger pigeons each year. You can't
find a single one now. We slaughtered the beaver and decimated
the buffalo herds. We obliterated the plains grizzly and reduced
the once common eastern mountain lion to little more than a
ghostly rumour.

Mind you, we haven't always killed our colleagues outright.
Sometimes we settled for simple animal humiliation. Tigers pacing
in cages, elephants balancing on balls. Bears in clown hats waltz-
ing to Strauss.

And all the while, the animals endured, with scarcely a cheep
or a hiss or a bellow of protest. Oh, once in a while a great white
picks off a surfer, a tiger snaps up a Bengali villager, or a Spanish
toro outfoxes a matador and pins him to the plaza sand — but tally
those paltry victories against, say, the number of Big Macs sold
each day.

No contest.

Ever since mankind began using his oversized brain to compensate for his undersized musculature, it's been a lopsided battle, but folks, I think the tide may be shifting. Something tells me the Big Referee in the Sky is about to start marking his scorecard in favour of the, um, underdogs.

Evidence? Purely circumstantial, so far. But read these three stories that appeared in the papers recently.

The first tale tells the plight of Troy Brewer, delivery boy for Domino's Pizza in Balch Springs, Texas. Troy's no greenhorn in the pizza delivery game. He's handled drunks, deadbeats, and no-shows.

But he draws the line at hold-up amphibians.

Late one Tuesday night, two rough-looking customers cornered Troy on a dark street. "Don't move," growled one as he drew his weapon from under his coat, "or yer gonna git bit." And there Troy was, nose to beak with a snapping turtle. "A big, huge, ugly one!" recalls Troy. "That sucker was gonna bite me!" The turtle-armed man escaped with about $50.

Scary, but not as scary as the story out of Fort Richey, Florida, where an outlaw gang is terrorizing a quiet, law-abiding community of peaceful retirees.

A gang of Muscovy ducks.

It's a big gang — at least a hundred members. In the past month alone, six residents have been assaulted. One woman had her dress chewed. Another man fell over a fence and cut his hand trying to escape. "They are mean," says one Fort Richey victim. "They keep after you. They get ugly and want to bite people."

My final animal horror story occurred right here in Canada, in Fairview, Alberta, as a matter of fact, where Donald Zenert decided to climb a fence into a deer enclosure to snap close-ups of some white-tailed does.

He apparently didn't notice the white-tailed buck.

Next thing Zenert knew, he was parrying antler thrusts from the infuriated male. And it was no bluff. "He was getting in some pretty good shots with his horns," says Zenert. "I figured the only way to keep him from putting an antler through my heart was to grab them and hang on."

So he did. For nearly two hours. He might still be there if the owner of the farm hadn't rescued him by shooting the buck.

Big deal, you say. Three unconnected stories, you say. Well, maybe. But I've been having nightmares about that Hitchcock movie, *The Birds*, recently.

And there was that owl hooting in the shopping mall.

All I can say is, if animals do take over the world, I trust the ants will put in a good word for me.

They better, after all the picnics I took them on.

For the Birds

T HAT MUST HAVE BEEN one highly unconventional turkey dinner
they celebrated down in Charlotte, North Carolina, this past
American Thanksgiving. Stuart and Terri Davis's Thanksgiving
dinner, I mean. Oh, there was turkey on the table, of course.
Actually, there were turkeys *at* the table. The Davises decided it
was high time that the most faithful attendees at Thanksgiving
dinner — which is to say the butterball gobblers that usually show
up for the feast headless, featherless, and lying drumsticks-up on
a platter — high time that the turkeys were shown a little respect.
So they served the usual stuffed squash, sweet potatoes, steaming
dinner rolls, and pungent pumpkin pie — but they served it *to* the
turkeys. Live ones, seated around the table. The Davises — who,
one gathers, do not exactly represent mainstream thinking in
North Carolina, which happens to be the number-one U.S. turkey
producer — say they wanted to protest farmers' treatment of the
birds.

Personally, I would've shown up in my best bib and tucker just
to hear grace. "Good food, good treats, gobba gobba, let's eat."

Well, who knows? Perhaps kindness to animals is an idea that
has finally come to roost in the human cranium. Seems to be the
case in Japan, where pets are babied to a degree that makes the
average North American dog and cat owner look like a Kentucky
muleskinner on a bad day. Water beds, flush toilets — even gold
jewellery are lavished upon pampered pooches and favoured
felines of Japan. They've even got their own line of compact discs.

Yep. Pet CDs. The reasoning (to stretch a word) goes like this. Your average Japanese pet-owning professional leads an unusually stressful life, right? Ten to twelve hours beating his or her brains out at the office. Battling like a hormone-besieged sockeye salmon through the torrents of traffic back to his house. Stands to reason that overstressed humans pass their frustrations on to their faithful four-legged companions when they finally wash up exhausted back at the ranch. Ergo: mood music for pets.

That's what they call the new aural offering: six slow and calm instrumental numbers on the doggie disc; seven somewhat bouncier and more rhythmic ditties for the kitties. "Cheerful and serene music is good for dogs," explains the veterinarian who created the discs, "while romantic music is best for cats."

Just in case your faithful companion is peering over your shoulder right now, you'd better warn him, her, or it that the Japanese are not soft and mushy about all forms of animal life.

Crows, for instance. Crows are a big problem in the Japanese town of Kisakata, gobbling up millions of yen worth of rice crops each year. So the Japanese have turned the tables. They are now trapping the crows and (gulp) eating them. "It tastes quite good," says the mayor of Kisakata, who is promoting crow meat as a local specialty.

Who knows? With a little soy sauce and a pinch of good press, the crow could become the butterball turkey of the Orient. And after the Orient? The poultry counter of our local supermarket, perhaps?

It's not impossible. These are the same people who took uncooked fish, redubbed it "sushi" and conned the rest of the world into lapping it up as a connoisseur's delight. Laugh if you will, but bear in mind . . . in a year or two you might be eating crow.

Bugs for Breakfast

I F YOU GET A DINNER invitation from Bruno Comby, phone him up right away and tell him you can't make it. Tell him your gerbil died, tell him your hair fell out, tell him you're having a stomach transplant that evening — tell him anything, but don't show up at his place at suppertime.

Unless you're a gastronomic adventurer of the first water.

Why? Well, Bruno Comby is author of a new book called *Insectes Délicieux*.

There now. You don't have to be Yves Fortier to figure out what the book's about, do you? *Delicious Insects*, we'd call it in English. Bruno Comby writes about the pleasures of eating bugs.

But before we croon "Yuk!" in two-part harmony, let's think about it for a moment.

Number one: we're obviously doing something wrong in the food department right now, because millions of people on the planet are going hungry.

Number two: vegetarians say that part of the problem is our addiction to meat. They have some telling statistics. Such as, the acre of land it takes to feed one calf could be used to raise 5,000 pounds of potatoes.

Ah, but that's several light years from sitting down to a plateful of creepy crawlies, isn't it? It's one thing to munch tofu burgers with a divot of alfalfa sprouts on the side; it's something else to face down a forkful of fricasseed cicada wings or french-fried June bugs.

185

But again, let's take a deep breath and think about it. Other cultures prize insects as rare taste treats. In Papua New Guinea, certain species of ants are the *pièce de résistance* at important feasts. In South Africa, moth caterpillars are considered a delicacy. Other cultures around the world lick their lips at the thought of locusts, flies, termites, and crickets.

"The idea of eating insects seems a little startling in a civilization where they are not eaten," writes Comby. That's putting it mildly, Bruno. Where I come from, the idea of eating insects is enough to get you tarred and feathered and ridden out of town on a Vapona No Pest strip.

It's blasphemous, but it's not unheard-of. There's a bottle of Mexican liqueur in my cupboard that has a larva floating around in the bottom of it. Right beside the bottle is a jar of jellied ants somebody gave me for my birthday last year.

Mind you, both of them are unopened.

Then there's the protein argument. Chicken is 23 percent protein. Locusts and grasshoppers contain a whopping 75 percent.

Which brings up another good reason for turning our knives and forks on insects: biologists acknowledge that insects are our biggest competitors for food and fibre, so why not cut out the middleman and go head to . . . antennae?

Consider: large swarms of locusts regularly strip crops in the Third World, bringing famine and death. Normally we call that a plague.

Why not call it dinner?

A large swarm containing 400 billion locusts would render down to nearly 10,000 tons of solid protein.

Besides, according to an Oregon University entomologist, we North Americans are already eating bugs — about two pounds' worth each, annually. The bugs are in our processed food, ground up into invisibly small chunks in everything from strawberry jam to frozen broccoli.

Why fight it? Heck, my front porch light attracts enough bugs to keep me in protein for a month or two. Then of course there's always pretty good pickin's on the car grille.

Sure! All it takes is an attitude change! Pass those candied bumblebees over here.

Whatsa matter? You've heard of humbugs, haven't you?

Sic 'Em, Mayor Bosco!

NOBODY ASKED, but if I had to name the most overrated critter on earth, I'd nominate the cockroach. Some folks go into a life-threatening coma when they discover cockroaches in their bathroom. What's the big deal? Cockroaches are tiny, they don't bark, scratch the furniture, or bite the mailman. Cockroaches take care of their own food and exercise requirements, don't carry fleas, and best of all, if your pet cockroach dies, who cares? There'll be 30 million replacements in the morning.

That's the scary factor with cockroaches, of course — their incredible fertility. Cockroaches make babies the way politicians make promises. They multiply so fast they make mink look like monks.

Which turns cockroaches into a very valuable commodity for newspaper editors. Any time there's a slow news day, your typical editor knows how to plug that ugly white cavity between the supermarket ad and the Help Wanted column. He or she just reaches for the Roach File and drags out a story detailing how the lowly cockroach, tougher than a leopard tank, more hyperactive than a lawyer's greed gland, able to leap tall, half-eaten peanut butter sandwiches in a single bound . . .

Is about to knock us all off our perch.

"COCKROACHES WILL
TAKE OVER PLANET"

is how the headline usually thunders. All I can say is: Aw, bullrushes.

The cockroach is no threat to us. Oh, I admit we humans are cruising for a crackup. You can't abuse a planet and its tenants the way we human landlords have and expect to get away with it forever. There's an eviction notice coming from Mother Nature some day soon. We are going to lose our number one rating in the Species Supremacy Sweepstakes all right — but it won't be cockroaches that knock us off.

It'll be dogs.

I know. I own one.

Sure, I grant you, he doesn't look like leadership material, lying on his back there in front of the chesterfield with his tongue lolling on the linoleum. His warrior potential is not immediately evident, but don't be fooled.

He's plotting. "Lying doggo," the Aussies call it. And he's not alone. All around the world, even as I type these words, Alsatians, dalmatians, wolfhounds and dachshunds, pit bulls and cockapoos are surreptitiously chewing through their leashes and tunnelling under Humane Society animal shelters. They've already memorized maps of fire hydrants and synchronized signals (one squirt if by land, two if by sea).

You don't believe me? You want proof? Exhibit A: *Doggie Adventure*. This is a movie, available at better video stores everywhere, detailing a day in the life of a dog. Viewers visit parks, city streets, a barnyard, and a couple of chow bowls. The difference between this and a rerun of "Lassie Come Home" is that *Doggie Adventure* is shot from a dog's perspective — which is to say, about a foot and a half off the ground. There's not much dialogue, but there's a lot of ambient sound — water being slurped, dog bones being crunched, hydro poles being sniffed and anointed, that sort of thing.

Doggie Adventure is a film not just about dogs. It's *for* dogs.

Still unconvinced there's a cur crusade in our future? Allow me to introduce the municipal leader of Sunol, California, a community in the San Francisco Bay area. Mayor Bosco was elected to office last spring.

It's difficult to say exactly what tilted the electorate in Mayor Bosco's favour. Mayor Bosco won't talk about his election strategy at all.

He can't. Talk about it, I mean. Mayor Bosco can only bark. He's a three-and-a-half-year-old black Labrador.

Today, Sunol, California, tomorrow perhaps a short dog trot up the coast to British Columbia, where history has shown that pretty well anything can be a provincial premier.

Trust me on this — the world is going to the dogs.

Go, Jays!

WHAT SHOULD WE TALK about today? Well, we could talk about the grain handlers' dispute. Or we could talk about constitutional amending formulas. Or we could stop pretending to be highbrow and talk about something really Canadian, topical and endlessly fascinating. The Blue Jays.

Relax, sir. Not those Blue Jays. The performers I want to chirp about are more hoarders than Borders; more carpers than Carters. They're a bunch of big Olerud boys from the family *Cyanocitta cristata*. Blue jays. The real blue jays. The ones with feathers. Unlike the baseball variety, real blue jays do not fly south when the season's over — they stick it out right through the winter around my place. You'll find 'em hunkered down from central Alberta all the way to Newfoundland's Avalon peninsula.

Truth to tell, blue jays don't hunker all that much. A lot of adjectives have been applied to this bird, but meek isn't one of them. Blue jays are kind of the buccaneers of the bird world. They're big, they're bold, they're brash, and they're not hard to spot. As a matter of fact, they're not hard to spot in a fog — because blue jays are yappy.

But fog or not, the blue jay comes dressed like a race track tout in his blue-black double-breasted, shiny spats, Cleopatra eyeliner, and a rakish crest combed up fit to make boxing promoter Don King . . . blue with envy.

I just watched a blue jay crash a bird feeder outside my window. He came in like a featherduster on amphetamines, landed with a squawk and a flourish, proceeded to chase off two chickadees and a purple finch, and then settled in to horse down not one sunflower seed, not a half dozen sunflower seeds. *Sixteen* sunflower seeds this feathered Electrolux syphoned into his crop before he lumbered unsteadily into the air and away. And he was back at the feeder within two minutes.

Blue jays don't eat from feeders the way normal birds do. They pillage them, then fly off to stuff the seeds in private stashes for later.

I haven't noticed any real blue jays flying around Blue Jay baseball games. Which is odd, considering the amount of popcorn that must get spilled there.

But it's probably just as well. A few years back, then-Yankee outfielder Dave Winfield totalled a seagull in Toronto's Exhibition Stadium. Couple of years after that, Atlanta Braves slugger Dion James stroked a fly ball to left field in Shea Stadium. It was a double for James, but strike three for a passing dove, which took the baseball amidships. Better the winged blue jays stay away from baseball games. Baseball stadiums are not bird-friendly.

Blue jays. They're on a feeding frenzy around my backyard feeders right now. Which is gratifying, given that there are no blue jays flocking on my TV screen anymore. The wingless, cloth-billed Blue Jays are gone for the season. I don't know where the human Jays migrate to each year in the late fall, but I hope they have bird feeders there. And I hope there are blue jays at the feeders. If the human Jays can learn to dominate a ball park the way real blue jays take over a bird feeder, and to gobble up grounders the way real blue jays siphon sunflower seeds — next year's World Series is in the bag again.

The Parrot
from Hell

HERE'S A TINY NEWS story out of Oslo, Norway, about a felon named Jokko. Jokko is in the slammer. His crime: aggravated assault. The judge figures Jokko's raucous behaviour contributed to a neighbour's heart attack. Jokko's sentence: one month behind bars. Jokko's jailhouse diet: sunflower seeds and water.

Jokko is a parrot.

You surprised that a judge could be so heartless as to send a parrot up the river? Not me. I'm not surprised that a parrot could cause a human to have a heart attack either. I've been there. You want a shaggy parrot story? Let me tell you about a parrot I once, it is to laugh, "owned."

I probably should have realized it would never work when the pet shop owner told me the parrot's name. There are a lot of fine parrot names. Jokko's not bad. Ruffles or Blue or Sinbad — those are all reasonable parrot monikers.

The Algonquin Round Table wit Dorothy Parker called her parrot Onan, because he constantly spilled his seed on the ground. I wasn't looking for anything that clever. "Polly" I could even have lived with.

But my parrot's name was Sydney. "Sydney the parrot" just doesn't work. It's like having a cheetah named Irving or a killer whale called Neil.

But Sydney it was. I paid the pet store owner an obscene amount of money for him, lashed out more bucks for mirrors and bells and toys and ladders and swings and special dietary supplements, plus a cage bigger than some of the apartments I rented in college.

And we went home, Sydney and I.

The pet store owner assured me that Sydney talked. That wasn't exactly true. Sydney screamed. He may have been saying words. They might even have been English. It's hard to say. You know how sound distorts once you get over 120 decibels.

I kept Sydney for three weeks. Twenty-one of the longest days of my life. During those twenty-one days Sydney pecked my cat, terrorized my dog, frightened my kids, drove away visitors. Trashed my living room. *And screamed.* Aside from standing next to a CF-18 jet fighter at full throttle, I don't think I've ever heard anything quite as eardrum-piercing as Sydney at full squawk.

When I found myself repeatedly thumbing through the Canadian Tire catalogue and lingering over the shotgun section, I knew it was time to admit defeat. I threw a bedsheet over Sydney's cage, detached it from the ceiling hook, and marched him back to the pet store owner. Who allowed as how he could maybe take the bird back as a favour, though not of course for anything like the price I'd paid. I can't prove it, but I swear out of the corner of my eye I caught reciprocal winks between Sydney and the pet shop guy.

Reminds me of the only shaggy parrot joke I know. Tall, impeccably dressed man walks into a bar with a beautiful Norwegian Blue perched majestically on his shoulder. The bartender's so impressed he drops the shot glass he's drying. "That's the most magnificent creature I've ever seen," the bartender cries. "Where'd you get it?"

"Him? Oh, Winnipeg, I think it was," says the parrot.

Parrot as Stool Pigeon

WHEN IT COMES TO FIDELITY, faithfulness, being true, standing by your man or woman . . . I'm with Honoré de Balzac. The famous French author was against the idea of philandery . . . fooling around. He thought one man ought to find more than enough to occupy himself with just one woman. "It is as absurd to say," said Balzac, "that a man can't love one woman all the time, as it is to say that a violinist needs several violins to play the same piece of music."

And yet . . . and yet . . .

There seems to be an awful lot of it going around. Infidelity, I mean. The scarlet letter shows up everywhere, from the sooty vests of chimneysweeps to the made-to-measure silk blazers of TV evangelists.

And Hollywood! We don't have time for an essay on infidelity in Hollywood. We don't even have time for the statistics. We don't even have time for Mae West's statistics.

Well, maybe we have time for a couple of Hollywood infidelity anecdotes.

The one about Zsa Zsa Gabor, for instance. Back before her cop-bopping days, the most famous Hungarian in Hollywood was famous for, well, getting married, and her apparent willingness to keep getting married until she got it right. Someone once asked her how many husbands she had had. Zsa Zsa looked baffled and replied, "You mean apart from my own dollink?"

Then there's the story of Chico, one of the famous Marx

brothers, who was kissing a chorus girl one day and got caught in the act. By his wife. Chico's defence, though highly creative under the circumstances, was on the whole rather lame. "I wasn't kissing her," protested Chico. "I was whispering in her mouth."

Ah, yes. The fear that makes honest partners of most of us, the fear of being blitzed and nailed if our eyes so much as stray beyond the corral.

Happened to Caesar and Cleopatra. Happened to Frankie and Johnnie. Happened to LiznEddienDicknDebbie. Happened to Carlos de Gambo. In a most peculiar way. Carlos was an Argentinian cad who fooled around. His faithful, long-suffering wife, Rosella, knew about it, and finally, thanks to Bozo, Rosella finally got the goods on Carlos. At the de Gambo divorce trial last year, Bozo took the stand to testify.

Or perhaps that should be . . . the perch to testify. Bozo is the de Gambos' pet cockatiel, and an eye-witness to the goings-on that went on in the de Gambo household whenever Señora de Gambo left the house.

"I knew he'd seen everything," explained Rosella. "He was using new words and giggling in a high female voice." At the trial the lawyers held an eight-by-ten glossy photo of one of Mr. de Gambo's glamorous visitors up before Bozo. "Honeybun, I love you," chirped Bozo. In answer to the prosecutor's question "Who loves Carlos?" Bozo the stool pigeon cockatiel squawked, "Ruby loves Carlos, Ruby loves Carlos." Ruby, alas, was the name of Carlos's secretary.

Bozo's testimony was allowed to stand, Carlos de Gambo is out on the street with a suitcase. Frankly, it doesn't surprise me. I doubt that even Chico Marx could have talked his way out of that one.

Philandering Fauna

I told my wife the truth: that I was seeing a psychiatrist. Then she told me the truth: that she was seeing a psychiatrist, two plumbers, and a bartender.

— Rodney Dangerfield

A DULTERY. "A sport created by the marriage system," according to one cynical wag. A sport that goes back a long way too, apparently. "An ancient and long-established custom . . . to set your neighbour's bed a-shaking." Who wrote that — Harold Robbins? Erica Jong? Irving Layton?

Nope. Those words were put together by a Roman scribbler by the name of Juvenal about two thousand years ago.

Oh well, at least the sin of adultery is confined to the human animal, right? *Homo sapiens* may be an inveterate two-timer, but the other species on the planet are simple, decent, honest types that stick with their mates no matter what.

Isn't that what the biology prof, *Reader's Digest*, and all those Walt Disney movies taught us?

Well, that used to be the way things were, Virginia. Up until just a few years ago, biologists believed that about 95 percent of all bird species were nuclear family types, one mother and one father sharing the burden of raising their brood. Lately, scientists have been looking a little more closely and discovering that those families aren't quite as squeaky-clean as they'd first thought.

In fact, they now estimate that up to a third of the birds in any given nest were probably sired by a, as the saying goes, "non-resident male."

And it's not just our feathered friends who are afflicted with the roving eye. Scientists have been shadowing rabbits, elk, and ground squirrels more closely than ever before.

Same story, basically. They've found that the aforementioned species fool around a lot more than we ever thought they did — and what's more, it's the females who usually initiate the debauchery.

As often as not, the male is reduced to a helpless, blustering cuckold, storming around kicking pine cones and cursing his in-laws while his inamorata is out painting the forest red with some other stud.

The male Idaho ground squirrel is particularly pathetic. When his mate is in heat, the male dogs her tirelessly right around the clock. He'll even chase her down a hole and sit on top of it to keep her away from any passing curly-tailed Casanovas.

As for birds, the experts are having trouble finding any feathered species that lives up to the old Puritan ethic. Even tiny chickadees, those chirpy, Audrey Hepburnish innocents who spend the winters with us, are not, it seems, immune to an illicit roll in the snow.

Philandering is rampant in the so-called animal world. Patricia Gowaty, a biologist at Clemson University, South Carolina, says, "It seems that all our old assumptions are incorrect."

Mind you, there may be a perfectly sound biological reason for all the extramarital matings these critters get up to. Experts theorize that the females may be ensuring that their eggs get fertilized by a variety of male donors, thus guaranteeing genetic diversity in her offspring.

Unlike humans, they don't do it just for fun.

Reminds me of the story of the old general who, off to the wars, locked his young wife in a chastity belt and gave the key to his best friend. "If I'm not back in a year, release my wife," said the general, and then he set off. That night in camp the general looked up to see his best friend galloping up to his tent. "General," he gasped, "you gave me the wrong key."

PART 6

Err . . . How's That Again?

Busted by the Lingo Police

WATCH YOUR MOUTH. The Lingo Police are everywhere. They don't wear badges and they don't carry revolvers, but they pack a lot of clout just the same. Lingo Police operate for the most part in Letters to the Editor columns and behind the shrubbery on university campuses. Description: earnest, strident, rigid, and utterly without humour. Avowed purpose: to root out and expose all examples of preferential language that leads to prejudice.

We're not just talking about racist slurs here. We're talking about institutions like Shakespeare. The fact that Shakespeare is revered perpetuates the subjugation of blacks and women. Why? Because Shakespeare was neither. Down with the Bard and his fellow dead white males.

Lingo police are also on constant "ism" alert. They watch for racism, elitism, ageism . . . and a couple I'd never heard of — sexism, of course, but heterosexism? That's the undue emphasis of heterosexuality as a sexual orientation.

Well, okay. But lookism?

Lookism is discrimination on the basis of looks. Now, simple human decency dictates that Roseanne Arnold has the same rights as Kim Basinger, and that Woody Allen gets to ride at the front of the bus with Tom Cruise. But to be correctly anti-lookist you must resist the urge to even notice any difference between Kim and Roseanne, Woody and Tom.

Then there's able-ism — that's oppression of the, what we used to call "handicapped" and our grandparents used to call "crippled." Both terms are verboten now. The only politically acceptable terminology is "differently abled." Thus, a person with no arms or legs who is blind, deaf, and mute is not handicapped — merely differently abled.

Just as I, who have no hair on my head, am not bald, just differently haired.

Does the madness ever end? Not so far as these differently abled eyes can see. In fact, it just keeps getting weirder.

The latest beachhead by the Lingo Police has left them in control of an American ecology magazine, *Earth Island Journal*. Recently, the journal printed a blacklist of phrases it calls "acutely embarrassing." Included are: "there's more than one way to skin a cat"; "chewing the fat"; "killing two birds with one stone"; and "dirt cheap." *Earth Island Journal* wants the expressions excised from the language.

Well, all I can say is, excuse me, officer, but that dog won't hunt. You may think language sanitation is easy as duck soup or shooting fish in a barrel, but I believe you will shortly find yourself marooned on the horns of a dilemma clutching a tiger by the tail.

You've loosed your dogs of war to defend a pig in a poke. You'd have to be blind as a bat and deaf as a coot to think your prissy commandments are any match for the enduring majesty of the English language. Dead white males like Shakespeare, Milton, Plato, and Aristotle will live on long after your feeble fiefdom is reduced to a dusty historical footnote. No offence, but you are backing the wrong horse and cannot see the forest for the trees.

Don't Judge a Livre by Its Cover

EVER BEEN REALLY, totally, utterly humiliated? Yeah, me too. I'm far too polite to ask about your experience, and still way too embarrassed to talk publicly about mine . . . so a compromise. I'll tell you all about Peter Van Harten's totally humiliating experience. Peter was a guy I went to school with. We also spent some time hoofing through Europe together. Now, Peter had a lot of swell personal attributes, but linguistic fluidity was not one of them. When it came to communicating in a foreign language, Peter might as well have been a goldfish.

I can see now that it was a terrible mistake to send him alone into that little grocery store in Calais. Get some eggs for breakfast, Pete, we told him. Les oeufs, s'il vous plait — that's all you have to say. And hold out your money.

Alas, Peter tried to finesse it. One should never try to finesse the French. Finesse is their business. Heck, finesse is their word.

"Ge vooks," announced Van Harten to the French grocer, "dez oofs de la pool . . ."

And that's as far as he got. A warp speed torrent of machine-gun French riding on a high, keening shriek erupted from the throat of Mme Defarge behind the counter. I didn't catch all of her rant as she drove Van Harten out into the street with her broom, but I know I heard "Quelle atroce!" — what an atrocity. There were some bits about never darkening doorways and barbarians from abroad too.

Well, the French are like that, eh? They love the language and they fuss and fret over the words of their language, treating them like preemies. Is there any other country that has a full-blown Academy meeting annually to decide whether new words are worthy enough to be admitted into the language? France does. A woman I know says she got a lot of glares whenever she spoke French in Paris. Which was disconcerting for her because she was from Trois-Rivières and had been speaking French all her life.

The French feel culturally superior to all mere mortals and make no bones about it. For years they've snickered at boorish Americans, patronized Québécois bumpkins, and twitted the Brits for their sang-froid. You just knew that they considered the rest of us unlettered brutes, and why not? Didn't our own literary standard-bearers — Callaghan and Hemingway and Joyce and Pound — answer the siren call of the Paris cafés? Ah, yes. France must truly be the most literary nation in the history of mankind.

Or so we all assumed until a study, commissioned by the French ministry of culture, came out. It shows that three-quarters of the French adults surveyed had never attended a classical music concert; over half had never seen a play, and two-thirds of them hadn't read *any* books recently.

Surprised? Me too. Serves us right, I guess, for making cultural assumptions about folks we don't know all that well. Reminds me of the story of an embassy dinner in Washington where a young American society woman sitting next to a Chinese dignitary tried to start a conversation by pointing to the entrée and saying, "Likee soupee?" The man nodded. After the meal the Chinese dignitary was asked to address the guests. Which he did. For ten minutes. In flawless English. Returning to his seat amid applause, he murmured to the young woman, "Likee speechee?"

Fractured English

HERE IS A LETTER from a grumpy reader that begins, "I have been several times surprised at your careless use of English, but you have outdone yourself in this . . ." And the letter goes on to flay me for an alleged linguistic misdemeanour.

All I can say to Grumpy Reader is, for God's sake, sir, obtain a life. If you have nothing better to do than pore over my poor prose winnowing out grammatical offences, then you are a man in serious need of a hobby.

Have you considered tatting?

Mind you, he has a point. English grammar and I have had little more than a nodding acquaintance since those dreary, dreadful days of Grade 7 English composition, when a merciless Miss Swinson lashed the class with volley upon volley of English Grammar Rules and Regs.

It made me the pathetic, unlettered wretch I am today. Even now, I shamble around with my participles dangling obscenely, tripping over misplaced modifiers, slapping ineffectively at insubordinate nouns, averting my eyes shyly from those brazen copulative conjunctions that don't even have the common decency to wear a set of brackets . . .

It's a situation up with which no one should have to put.

And sometimes I can't — put up with it, I mean. When that happens I have a failsafe cure. I reach for my Fractured English file.

This is where I keep my collection of pieces by people who

mangle the English language even more grievously than I (do). More often than not, these folks are labouring under a disadvantage — namely, that English is clearly not their first language.

Such as whoever wrote this brochure for a Japanese car rental firm. Some advice it offers: "When a passenger of foot heave in sight, tootle the horn. Trumpet at him melodiously at first, but if he still obstacles your passage, then tootle him with vigour."

Or these assembly instructions that came with an Italian-made baby carriage: "Insert the blushing for blocking in the proper split, push it deeply and wheel in anti time sense till it stops."

Oh yes, and *buona fortuna*. I believe that's Italian for good luck.

A polite reminder on the back of a Japanese hotel room door is, I think, appropriately Zen-like: "Is forbitten to steal the hotel towels please. If you are not person to do such thing, is please not to read notis."

In the Scandinavian countries, English is often spoken, but not always flawlessly. Witness the Oslo cocktail lounge that sports a sign reading: "Ladies are requested not to have children in the bar."

Riding in elevators can be unnerving in the most cosmopolitan of cities, but there's one lift in Belgrade that I intend to avoid for the rest of my life. It carries a sign that reads in (sort of) English: "To move the cabin, push button for wishing floor. If the cabin should enter more persons, each one should press number of wishing floor. Driving is then going alphabetically by national order."

Under which some wag has crayoned: "Or you could take the stairs."

Sometimes overseas English isn't merely mangled — it's fraught with menace. Look at this advertisement in a Hong Kong dentist's window. It reads: "Teeth extracted by the latest Methodists."

Or the sign in a Jordanian tailor shop that advises: "Order your summer suit. Because is big rush we will execute customers in strict rotation."

Or the notice on the wall of an Acapulco hotel dining room: "The management has personally passed all the water served here."

No wonder they warn *turistas* not to drink the water.

No Name like a Brand Name

STEPHEN LEACOCK defined advertising as "the art of arresting the human intelligence long enough to get money from it." George Orwell was less kind. "Advertising," said Orwell, "is the rattling of a stick inside a swill bucket." Sounds to me like two men who were unduly jangled by jingles, but Leacock and Orwell were nothing if not professional. Even they would have to admit that advertising, if it has to be done, should at least be done well.

Which brings us to the subject of brand names, and why some of them leap right up, bite you in the eye, and cling to the mind like treble-hook fishing lures, while others elicit little more than a yawn or a ho-hum on their downward spiral to advertising oblivion.

Some brand names are breathtakingly dumb. Others are positively ingenious. Take Spic and Span. Can you think of a better name for a household cleanser? It's short, easy to remember, and evocative. Just about perfect. Which is probably why Spic and Span's been around so long.

Now, Xerox shouldn't be successful as a brand name. It's wrong because as a word it's meaningless. Plus, it calls for the larynx of a bullfrog to pronounce properly (Gzzzerox) . . .

As a brand name, Xerox is all wrong, but the people at Xerox, by dint of lashing out millions of advertising dollars, have made it *all right*. They managed to transform what sounds like a Martian burp into an English noun and verb meaning "copy." We now talk blithely of xeroxing this or getting a xerox of that.

Alas, success went to Xerox's corporate head. A few years ago Xerox bought up a computer company and began marketing a line of Xerox computers. The public stayed away in droves. Why? Because Xerox, in the public mind, means copy, not computer. Those original ad campaigns had done their work too well.

Other brand name disasters? How about Pierre Cardin wines? Bic perfume? The Swatch car? Believe it or not, they've all been floated, briefly and disastrously, over the past few years by hopeful marketing gurus. They all sank like stones to the bottom of Orwell's swill bucket.

And if you were very observant down at the corner store last year you might have caught the almost split-second birth, life, and death of Life Savers Gum. Yes, the manufacturers of Life Savers tried unsuccessfully to crack the chew market with their own brand of gum. Nobody bought it. That's because to several generations of sweet-toothed consumers, the Life Saver is and ever will be a tiny doughnut-shaped candy (except on airplanes where it's a personal flotation device — but that's another advertising story).

Ah, it's a relentless business, advertising. They never let up. "Tell 'em quick and tell 'em often," advised William Wrigley, the Chiclet King. He might have added, "Tell 'em big." Joseph Pulitzer believed in that. The one-time owner of the New York *Evening World* once removed his Havana from his mouth long enough to tell his advertising staff that he wanted a billboard advertising his newspaper to be erected in New Jersey. And he wanted that billboard to be big, big enough to be visible from Mars. There was a long silence, then one of the advertising men piped up: "Ah, Mr. Pulitzer, sir . . . what language should the sign be printed in?"

I like to think the moment was followed by at least thirty seconds of noncommercial silence.

What's the Fuss?

I GIVE UP. I figured that after forty-nine years I had maybe figured out a thing or two about life and how it works, but I was wrong. Once again Life has blown right by me like a Nolan Ryan forkball, and I've been left swinging like a batwing door.

Life's latest puzzlement: the Benetton brouhaha.

Benetton, for those of you who don't follow fashion, is an Italian clothing company, as famous for its oddball advertising campaigns as it is for the apparel it merchandises. They've sponsored billboards showing a priest kissing a nun. They've featured full-page magazine spreads in which a little white girl kisses a little black boy.

But now the ad lads at Benetton have gone too far — for the British, anyway. The inhabitants of Blighty awoke one morning not long ago to find their country speckled with Benetton billboards of the most obscene and offensive nature. Radio and television station switchboards were inundated with calls from outraged citizens. Letters that began "I was shocked and appalled" fell in blizzard-like drifts on the rounded shoulders of newspaper editors. The British Advertising Standards Authority fielded more than eight hundred calls demanding the billboards be covered over instantly.

Cause of the abomination? Photos of mutilated corpses, perhaps? Close-ups of tortured hamsters? Ethiopian refugees? Mike Wallace without makeup?

No.

210

Benetton incensed the British public by showing a newborn child, complete with umbilical cord, on its billboards.

"It has caused a very large amount of distress to the public," according to the director general of the Advertising Standards Authority.

In the name of sanity, why? We accept *Robocop*, *Terminator*, and *Friday the Thirteenth* movies. We don't blink at newsreels that show Iraqi conscripts being ionized by Stealth bombers. We gobble up westerns, the Superbowl, and "Fight Night Live" from Las Vegas . . .

But we can't handle the sight of a newborn baby?

We had another example of this strange new sensitivity a while back when *Vanity Fair* hit the stands. There on the front cover was a shot of a Hollywood star from the waist up. She was facing to the left, turning with a coy smile towards the camera. And she was naked.

Nothing unusual in that. Every week the newsstands are blanketed with magazines that feature naked cover girls in poses that range from corny cheesecake to hard-core porn.

But there was something daringly, utterly different about the *Vanity Fair* cover. The star was the actress Demi Moore.

And she was defiantly, triumphantly pregnant.

I can't recall such pandemonium over a periodical since *Time* magazine asked "IS GOD DEAD?" in big bold letters on its cover about twenty years back. Late-night comedians cracked jokes about the pregnant cover girl. Radio and TV talk shows debated whether the editors of *Vanity Fair* had the "right" to publish such a shot.

Again, what's the big deal? How can a simple and tasteful shot of a woman with child upset folks as jaded as we are?

Two of the most beautiful things I know in this world are newborn babies and barrel-bellied mothers-to-be.

Makes you wonder what would happen if Joseph and Mary tried to book a room in the Jerusalem Inn nowadays. They'd probably give them a room, all right.

As long as Mary didn't mind being X-rated.

But First a Word from Our Sponsor

WHAT A CURIOUS BEAST is this thing called advertising. It is, by and large, a phenomenon of our times. Nineteenth-century Canadians didn't have — or need — full-page magazine ads or thirty-second TV spots to tell them They Deserved a Break Today or when it was Time for a Blue. We are not so fortunate. There's probably not a Canadian alive who can remember a time when he or she was not being exhorted to buy a carton of this or a six-pack of that. We are the consumer society, born to shop till we drop and buy till we die.

It's pervasive and, like the hole in the ozone, it seems to get bigger every year. I don't know about you, but I hardly watch any TV these days. Not since the advertising breaks got to be longer than the program segments.

Other media aren't much better. Have you bought a copy of the Toronto *Star* recently? It's Canada's largest paper, and if you ever run up against a Saturday edition you'll have no trouble believing it. It looks like a copy of a normal paper following an overdose of steroids. You practically need a wheelbarrow to get the monster from the newsstand to your easychair. But the thing is, it's mostly advertising! Take out the flyers, the circulars, the full-page spreads for appliances and supermarket specials, the real estate section, the classified section, the travel bumf, and the used car listings — and you won't have enough editorial content to fill the belly button of a cub reporter.

Newspapers like the *Star* are misnamed. They should be called adpapers.

Oh well, as my uncle (he's with the prestigious law firm Sue, Grabbit, and Runne) says: "Don't knock it, sonny — advertising makes the world go round."

I suppose he's right. I just wish advertisers were a little classier about it.

Have you heard, for instance, about the latest frontier to be cracked by advertisers?

It's grooming products. For children.

Seriously. Hair shampoo, conditioners, sunblock, moisturizing lotions, liquid soaps, after-bath powders — that sort of thing — aimed strictly at upscale infants and trendy toddlers.

Right now, the advertisers are engaging in a little pre-emptive psychological warfare, softening up the resistance they expect to get when they start targeting a consumer group that hasn't even hit puberty yet. The ad boys are calling their pre-pubescent product line "developmentally appropriate." They're insisting that vanity products will "instill a sense of personal pride in children." Goodies such as Wild Grape Body Shampoo Gel will, they say, make kids feel special and enhance their self-esteem.

Sure. And if pigs had wings, advertisers would figure out a way to sell them flight insurance.

Well, after all, this is the industry that gave us vaginal deodorant and basketball shoes that pump themselves up. Like most voracious parasites, advertising constantly needs new hosts to feed off. Kiddy exploitation is just a natural progression, I guess. But it bums me out. And the next time I enter a department store I'll be humming a version of that old John Donne line:

"Ask not for whom the cash register tolls, it tolls for thee. And thy kids."

Tabloids and Ethics: A Natural Oxymoron

You cannot hope to bribe or twist
thank God! the British journalist
but seeing what the man will do
unbribed, there's no occasion to.

— Humbert Wolfe

SOMETIMES I THINK I'd like to visit England just for the thrill of strolling down to a London newspaper kiosk and browsing through the morning headlines. One of the few fine remaining pleasures of life in that sad and shabby kingdom is the range of newspapers you can peruse. For a modest mittful of newpence you can take your choice of anything from the august London *Times* at the upscale end all the way down to scuzzy, unspeakable typographical excrescences like the *Mirror* and the *Sun*. For a journophile like yours truly, reading the British press is like living in a lovely English garden overlooking a garbage dump.

The best of British journalism is unquestionably very good indeed. But the worst, my dears, is among the very worst in the world. If you haven't stained your fingers on a typical British tabloid, then you don't know how low the fourth estate can stoop. Canadian tabloids are flashy, irreverent, and occasionally outrageous, but Canadian tabs are to British tabs as a Brownie pack is to the Mongol hordes.

Few institutions can be as mindlessly chauvinistic or stupefyingly sexist as a British tabloid newspaper in full screech. They flay the royal family unmercifully, insinuating that Prince Charles is an airhead and Princess Margaret a souse. They publish full-page photos of naked nymphets, complete with slavering, sleazy captions about "Luscious Lily's garden of natural delights." There are five basic staples for a classic British tabloid item: sex, soccer, sex, scandal, and sex. And if you can throw in a pinch of aristocratic philandery, you've got yourself a front-page byline, mate.

All of which made me do a serious double take when I saw this headline in my non-British, non-tabloid copy of the *Globe and Mail*. U.K. TABS SIGN ETHICS CODE, it read.

British tabloids? An ethics code? That's like Mike Tyson becoming a Buddhist.

Under the new code, British newspapers will have to justify their intrusions into private lives, mistakes will be acknowledged in print with the same prominence the original items enjoyed, and henceforth editors will no longer pay criminals, their families, or their associates for rights to their "stories."

All of which sounds very laudable, but adherence to the code is strictly voluntary. There's no law that will force any newspaper to actually follow through and obey the code.

You will forgive an old cynic for suspecting that it will be a frosty Friday on Fleet Street before the editors of the *Sun* or the *Mirror* send their reporters out with the gentle admonition to be fair, gentle, and upright at all times.

I prefer to believe that the British press will continue to offer the bewildering and occasionally revolting kaleidoscope of journalism that it has always served up. A full spectrum — good, bad, and ugly — that has been deftly summarized in this excerpt from the book *Yes, Prime Minister*, by Jonathan Lynn and Anthony Jay:

"The *Times* is read by the people who run the country. The *Daily Mirror* is read by the people who think they run the country. The *Guardian* is read by the people who think they ought to run the country. The *Morning Star* is read by people who think the country ought to be run by another country. The *Independent* is read by people who don't know who runs the country but are sure they're doing it wrong. The *Daily Mail* is read by the wives of the people who run the country. The *Financial Times* is read by the people who own the country. The *Daily Express* is read by the people who think the country ought to be run as it used to be run. The *Sun*'s readers don't care who runs the country provided she has big boobs."

Coming in on a Wing and an Eponym

LET'S TAKE A BRIEF stroll through the garden of eponyms . . . which is to say, names that became words. They're every-where, eponyms. From the Stetson on your brow to the Levi's on your backside. (John B. Stetson, Philadelphia hatmaker; Levi Strauss, San Francisco overall manufacturer.)

And not just clothes. We've got eponyms in the air (Learjet, Lockheed); eponyms on the dinner table (Caesar salad, Porter-house steak, peaches Melba); we have, for crying out loud, eponyms on the thermometer (Gabriel Fahrenheit and Anders Celsius).

Becoming an eponym can be quite glorious if you're a Merce-des or a Benz, a Rolls or a Royce. Or it can be rather grisly if you're Dr. Joseph Guillotine or British artillery officer Henry Shrapnel. But let's not linger in the grim sector . . . that would be Marquis de Sadistic. Let us turn instead to the loopy side of eponyms.

How would you like to be remembered forever as a pair of tights? That was the fate of Jules Leotard. Cheer up. You could have been a Kentucky distiller by the name of E. S. Booze. Or perhaps the Britisher who gave the world the modern ceramic toilet bowl. A chap with the unfortunate moniker of Thomas Crapper.

Never mind. It might have been worse even that that. Fate might have dealt you the passport held by the personal physician to King Charles III. Life should have been sweet for that esteemed gentleman. He lived in a time when Shakespeare's plays premièred just down the street. He was handsome, well spoken, more than competent — knighted, in fact, for his skill. Alas, he served a monarch who, not to dwell on it, fooled around. A lot. Chuck Three was a philanderer and majesterially concerned about picking up venereal disease. Charles instructed his physician to come up with a device that would allow His Majesty to pursue his extracurricular activities without jeopardizing the crown jewels, as it were.

The physician sighed and went away and did his duty. Came up with just the ticket — a sheath of oiled sheep's intestine. And what did the doctor get for his devotion? A chestful of gold? An estate in Hampton? A fistful of shares in the Hudson's Bay Company? An afternoon with Nell Gwynn? Naw. The physician got just what he feared most. Immortality through his venereal intervention invention.

Did I mention the physician was the Earl of Condom?

I guess it's just as well the Earl's no longer with us. He'd never give credence to what three and a half centuries and an AIDS scare have done to his little device. Would he ever believe that sleepy downtown London, Ontario, has a Condomery — a kind of Sheik boutique or safe supermarket? Would the Earl believe that the manufacturers of the U.S. Stealth bomber are currently suing makers of the Stealth condom because the condoms are sold in a cardboard carton replica of the bomber, which, the planemakers claim, constitutes trademark infringement? Would the Earl of Condom believe that? I can hardly believe it myself, but it's true. Personally, I think the bomber manufacturers are overreacting. They ought to welcome Stealth condoms with open wingflaps. Especially the Stealth condom sales slogan, "They'll never see you coming."

You just can't buy advertising like that.

Sanitized English Spoken Here

I SEE WHERE THE LOBLAWS supermarket chain is yanking a brand of its tortilla chips off the shelf. It's a name problem. The chips are called Suicide Blues. Loblaws says it has received letters denouncing the brand name as "offensive and insulting."

I'm trying to get my mind around this latest outbreak of self-censorship fever. What's the problem here? Are we concerned that some late-night customer, teetering on the edge of mental stability, will spy a snack pack of Suicide Blues in the local 7-Eleven, snap, and end it all right there at the checkout counter?

Could happen, I guess. But how far is the marketplace willing to go to save one nameless manic depressive? Will Labatt's Blue disappear from the beer stores? Would Black's Photography be keen on changing their name to Sunny's Snapshots?

How far might this go? Would "Hockey Night in Canada" be persuaded to drop the concept of sudden death overtime? I guess the card game blind man's bluff would be verboten.

Silly? Sure, it's silly — but no sillier than some of the other word games that are actually going on right now, all in the name of Political Correctness. PC is still the rage on university and college campuses. What it amounts to is troops of self-appointed volunteer Thought Police deciding what is and isn't politically correct for the rest of us to think and say. Thus, a Harvard Dean recently condemned members of his university dining-room staff for holding a "Back to the Fifties" party. Reason? Because he deemed it Politically Incorrect to honour a decade that was marred by

219

segregation. Thus, an official at the University of California campaigns to ban phrases like "a chink in one's armour" or "a nip in the air" because words like "chink" and "nip" could be misconstrued as racial epithets.

But you don't have to stumble through the minefields of the groves of academe to find correctional goon squads at work. Cripples, paraplegics, and amputees no longer dwell among us. Now, there are only the physically challenged. Well, yes, I agree a person with, say, no arms or legs is physically challenged, but the term is rather vague. After all, a person with bunions or thirty pounds of body fat, or a lush trying to navigate an expressway with a snootful of bar rye, is physically challenged too. English is a wonderful linguistic quiver brimful of thousands of very sharp, very precise adjectival arrows. We oughtta use the right shaft whenever we can.

My beef with the Political Correction Police is that their prime concern is sanitation, not honesty. Give 'em their head and they'll be knitting veils and crocheting lace doilies for Shakespeare.

Politically correct speech? Naw. Give me straight talk every time.

How Do You Spell Relief?

L ET US, GENTLE READER, you and I, divert our gaze from the pressing questions of the day. Let Peter Mansbridge juggle the crisis in the Gulf. Leave Pamela Wallin to empathize on the airwaves about the GST, the limping loonie, and the ups and downs of the Rafferty-Alameda. Not for us a searing exposé of death on the highways or suspected life in Ottawa. Let us instead turn our jaded senses to the plight of Denise Wells. She went before the Gods of Justice in Houston, Texas, just an eyeblink ago.

Her alleged crime: going to the washroom. Not long ago, Ms. Wells attended a country music concert. Like most popular concerts, this one attracted a crowd. And crowds mean lineups. Lineups for tickets, lineups for hotdogs, lineups for soft drinks, and lineups, inevitably, for the washroom. Denise Wells lined up for the washroom. For a while. Then she noticed an infuriating thing.

She noticed that the lineup for the washroom with the humanoid stick woman over the door stretched out slightly longer than the Rio Grande. Whereas the lineup for the washroom with the humanoid stick *man* over the door was nonexistent! No lineup. Denise Wells stood it for as long as she could stand it, then she did something that, when you think of it, it's amazing more women don't do all the time.

She said the heck with it and went in the men's washroom.

Why not? She wasn't hooking or dealing coke or selling nuclear submarine blueprints to the Iraqis. She only wanted to go to the bathroom!

She was arrested just the same, and charged under a gothic Houston city ordinance that forbids using public washrooms for members of the opposite sex in a manner calculated to cause a disturbance.

Which is dumb. Ms. Wells would have created a much more annoying disturbance if she hadn't availed herself of the men's facilities, but that's hypocritical par for the course when it comes to public conveniences.

We're such a bunch of goody-goody two-Guccis when it comes to the everyday unisexual common denominator of taking a leak. You come to my house, we use the same toilet. I go to your house, we use the same toilet. But go to a restaurant, a school, an airport, or a shopping mall and suddenly it's Dick and Jane at the Mackenzie King Junior Public School — separate facilities, puh-leeze.

Even the wishy-washy words we still use! The privy, the loo, the potty, the necessary, the *water closet*. Not to mention restroom, washroom, bathroom. We do not want to bathe. We don't want to wash, and we don't want to rest. We want to go to the can.

As did Denise Wells — who is very classy, as public urinators go. When the police hauled her away she yelled, "Hey, fellas, I left the seat up, just the way you like it."

Reminds me of the story of the great wit Dorothy Parker, who, sitting at her customary spot at the Round Table in the Algonquin Hotel, announced, "I have to go to the bathroom."

On her way out she tossed over her shoulder, "Actually, I want to use the telephone, but I was too embarrassed to say so."

I don't know if they got the joke at the Round Table, but Denise Wells would.

Judicious English

SOMEBODY ONCE DEFINED A JUDGE as a person of few words but many sentences. Well, you can read that verdict any way you like. The fact is that judges — and justice in general — remain firmly in the realm of mystery for most of us.

I think language is largely to blame. The system of jurisprudence that governs our lives springs from a bedrock of Latin. Now that was hunky-dory when young scholars lapped up Latin and Greek at the feet of their school instructors. Nowadays, kids are more likely to be taking advanced computer graphics and conversational Mandarin. People are moving along with the times. But the law clings tenaciously to its Latin roots. Now, Latin may or may not be a dead language, but it's certainly buried. Which becomes a problem when life throws one of its wicked split-fingered fastballs at us and we find ourselves in a court of law. Suddenly the air is full of *ipso facto*s and *flagrante delicto*s. We hear strangers droning on about *mandamus* and *mittimus*. They tell us it's a case of Regina *versus* Black and it will be held *in camera*.

And most of us don't have a clue what they're talking about.

Jim Carnwath is somebody who would like to change all that by bringing our judicial system into the twentieth century, linguistically speaking. And that's good news for the rest of us, because Jim Carnwath is a Provincial Court judge.

Each year Judge Carnwath drives down to London, Ontario, for a couple of weeks in the summer and stands up in front of a classroom, not a courtroom, of fellow judges. And that's when

Judge Carnwath really begins his mission: to teach his colleagues to speak English.

Common, ordinary, over-the-back-fence, down-at-the-Legion-Hall English. Mostly he's trying to get the judges to shed their fondness for abstruse windiness and stuffy legalisms. He encourages them to forgo intoning "cease and desist" when what they mean is "stop." As he puts it: "Who would ever come home for dinner and say, 'I'd like another piece of that raspberry pie. Said pie was the best you ever made.'?"

He tells them to get rid of the *ab initio* — the phrase "in the beginning" is much clearer. Similarly, he tells the judges to stop referring to the *actus reus* when what they mean is "the criminal act."

More power to Judge Carnwath, I say. Still, I hope he doesn't take all the wind out of those judges' linguistic sails. There are occasions when judicial obfuscation is called for. Such as the time one Alberta circuit court judge had to write to a British couple informing them that their young son had been found guilty and hanged for cattle rustling. The judge didn't *have* to be compassionate, but he saw no reason to compound the parents' grief by telling them their son had ended a dissolute life at the end of a rope. So he took plumed pen in hand and wrote: "Please accept my condolences on the loss of your son. His youth was cruelly snatched from him when a platform on which he was standing suddenly gave way."

Not strictly honest, perhaps . . . but judicious in the finest sense of the word.

Get Out of My Emergency Room

YOU WOULD THINK THAT a day that begins with a guy opening a bus terminal door in a clumsy enough fashion to rip the nail off his second biggest toe, which is sticking out of the open-toed sandal on his right foot . . . you would think that a day that begins that way will probably have nothing good about it — but not so. I managed to mangle my foot just that way not so long ago, and as a result I wound up learning a good chunk of an entirely new language.

Wrecking my foot got me into the hospital emergency waiting room. At first I was like everyone else in there — an impatient patient quite absorbed in my personal world of pain and haemmorrhage. But as the hours rolled on and I waited my turn and the bleeding stopped and the throbbing subsided, I began to hear things beyond my own shallow breath, beyond the coughs and clichés and complaints of my stricken fellows. I began to hear the language of the hospital. Crisp professionals in white coats flitting by, speaking, as they went, fluent medicalese.

One of the first things I learned in medicalese was "blue pipe." My foot injury, as much as it smarted, wasn't serious because I hadn't hit a blue pipe. "Blue pipe?" I peeped. "No, it was a big heavy aluminum door down at the bus ter—" The admitting nurse laughed. He explained that blue pipe means artery. I hadn't cut an artery. Heck, I hadn't even nicked a *red* pipe — you know, a vein.

"What's wrong with her?" I murmured, shifting my eyes laterally to a fussily dressed woman on the other side of the waiting room. "Not a thing," he hissed. "She's strictly a gomer. We're going to buff her up and turf her."

Gomer? Buff? Turf? Well, "turf" is pretty obvious, my informant told me. To "buff up" a patient is to get her ready to leave the hospital.

And Gomer?

"Gomer," he said, "is a doctor's term for patients who waste our time. G.O.M.E.R.: Get Out of My Emergency Room."

Oh, I learned a lot, waiting for someone to treat the ground chuck that once was my toe. I learned that patients can be bronked and cathed and zapped. Being bronked is examination by bronchioscope. Cathed is being fitted for a catheter. Zapped refers to electroshock therapy. Patients can also be bagged or boxed. Being bagged is better. That's when a nurse gives you oxygen manually. Being boxed, well . . . that's the box they put you in when bronking, cathing, zapping, and bagging have all failed.

I learned that though I'd lost a toenail and would probably take a stitch or two, at least my foot wasn't bubar — which is to say, Buggered Up Beyond All Repair.

Survival tips, too. Next time I visit a hospital I shall try very hard to remember not to exhibit the dreaded O sign (head back, mouth open) or worse still, the Q sign (head back, mouth open, tongue lolling out). But I hope not to need that knowledge anytime soon. If you and I should meet at the bus terminal, I'd appreciate it if you held the door open. I'll be easy to spot — the guy in the steel-toed sandals. Who answers to the name Gomer.

Oxymorons I Have Known

BREAK OUT THE PLASTIC glasses and fill 'em up with nonalcoholic wine. Serve up those fresh frozen jumbo shrimp and pass the diet candy. It's time to launch a brand-new tradition. We could call it the First Annual Oxymoron Hunt. And how ya doin' so far? I mean, you and I are old acquaintances and I've already flung, lemme see, one two three four five six seven . . . eight of 'em at you. Oxymorons, I mean. It's a word that comes from a couple of Greek words, one meaning sharp, the other meaning dull — "pointedly foolish," if you will. My *Shorter Oxford* (kind of an oxymoron itself) defines "oxymoron" as the conjunction of incongruous or contradictory terms, such as mournful optimist. As I said, we also have plastic glasses, nonalcoholic wine, fresh frozen, jumbo shrimp, diet candy, new tradition, first annual, and should old acquaintance be forgot . . . that's one too.

Oxymorons. Don't get too close, they're contagious. Venerable as well. Shakespeare toyed with oxymorons. Remember Romeo nattering on about love?

> *O brawling love! O loving hate!*
> *O anything! Of nothing first create!*
> *O heavy lightness! serious vanity!*

Well, Romeo was a love-struck puppy at the time. What do you expect?

Milton was sober as a judge when he wrote about being darkly wise and rudely great. Tennyson got off a particularly wicked oxymoron about Lancelot:

"His honour rooted in dishonour stood
And faith unfaithful kept him falsely true."

Ah, they don't write poetry like that anymore — but we're still cranking out oxymorons, some of them great.

I think it's hard to improve on giant economy size, black light posters, or classic rock. Has any other generation been able to buy products that are *both* new and improved? Wear clothes that leave one barely dressed? Read faxes that are stamped "original copy"?

And would Shakespeare, Milton, or Tennyson ever have guessed that one day the world's greatest single source of oxymorons would turn out to be . . . the military? Sure. The folks who gave us war games. Peace offensive. Routine evacuation. And the absolutely untoppable civil war.

Chalk it up to another oxymoron: military intelligence.

There is one other branch of human endeavour that gives us plenty of if not classic oxymorons at least pointedly foolish observations. That branch is politics. And Canadians are among the front runners. It was Mackenzie King who stunned the nation with "Not necessarily conscription but conscription if necessary." It was a retiring Trudeau who said, "I was my best succesor, but I decided not to succeed myself." It was Mulroney who single-handedly turned the phrase "sacred trust" into an oxymoronic kiss of death.

Let me leave you with the only economic oxymoron I know: "It should be noted that a slowing up of the slowdown is not as good as an upturn in the downcurve, but a good deal better than either a speedup of the slowdown or a deepening of the downcurve; and it does suggest that the climate is about right for an adjustment to the readjustment."

I tell ya. How Mazankowski beat me out for Finance, I'll never know.

Able Was I, Ere I Saw Palindromes...

I SNAGGED THE JANGLING TELEPHONE on the third ring and stuck it next to my good ear. The voice inside claimed to be calling from a magazine called *Prairie Fire*, in Winnipeg. The voice wanted to know if I would be willing to judge palindromes. I laughed harshly. "I'm sorry," I snapped, "I admit I've done a lot of damnfool things in my life — I've kayaked on whitewater, accepted a blind date in Moose Jaw, eaten dinner in a place called Mom's — even delivered an after-dinner speech unarmed to a roomful of B.C. lawyers. I may be reckless, but I'm not an out and out fool. I do not get involved in exotic animal contests!"

The voice on the phone was patient, cajoling. It explained that a palindrome is not a critter, it's a literary construction. What makes a palindrome is that it reads the same no matter which end you start at.

"Mom" is a very simple palindrome. So is "dad." And "Otto" and "Anna." Slightly more complex palindromes include "radar" and "level."

Then you get to the real beauties, such as Adam's introductory come-on to Eve:

Madam, I'm Adam.

And Napoleon's purported lament as he stared out to sea from his island exile at the end of his career:

Able was I ere I saw Elba.

Not to mention what could have been the advertising slogan for the construction of the most famous canal on the planet:

A man, a plan, a canal — Panama!

Actually, the last example, though ingenious, is not a true palindrome. There's a dastardly dash in there that mucks up the symmetry. But you get the idea. I got the idea. I told the voice on the phone I would be delighted to judge *Prairie Fire*'s palindrome contest.

Within a few days my faithful Canada Post mailperson was staggering up the front steps to my door, bowed nearly double under the weight of contest entries. I attempted to regale him with the lewdest palindrome I'd come across:

Eros, Sidney, my end is sore!

He was not amused. I distinctly heard a *sotto voce* snarl in both official languages.

There were some dandy palindromes in the package he left behind. Dave Wright sent in a taunt for the butcher of Baghdad:

Mad dash, eh Saddam?

Myra Stilborn offered:

IOU 'n' UOI

— with a footnote that read: "Palindromic licence allows grammatical freedom (me hope)."

And this rather magnificent Peter/Glenda Rogers collaboration:

Draw a dahlia, my revered nude man. (named under) Every mail had award.

There, but for a slight vagueness and a pair of rogue brackets, would be my prize winner.

In any case, half the Rogers palindromic tag team won. I awarded first prize to Peter Rogers for his instructions on the boarding of errant wilderness hunters:

Room a nimrod at a dorm in a moor.

How about you? Want to try your luck at writing palindromes? Then write 'em down and send them in, care of Stoddart Publishing.

But no rush. I don't want to hurry you, so let's make a palindromic cut-off date. Let's say your palindromes don't have to reach me for the next few years.

Or, to be precise, by 20/02/2002.